Brandfather

JOHN MURPHY
THE MAN WHO INVENTED
BRANDING

The Book Guild Ltd

First published in Great Britain in 2017 by
The Book Guild Ltd
9 Priory Business Park
Wistow Road, Kibworth
Leicestershire, LE8 0RX
Freephone: 0800 999 2982
www.bookguild.co.uk
Email: info@bookguild.co.uk
Twitter: @bookguild

Typeset in Minion Pro

Printed and bound in the UK by TJ International, Padstow, Cornwall

ISBN 978 1911320 357

British Library Cataloguing in Publication Data.
A catalogue record for this book is available from the British Library.

To Janet

ACKNOWLEDGEMENTS

About twelve years ago I was approached by my friend and former colleague Andy Milligan to write an account of the setting up of Interbrand and of its first twenty years; this was the period up to 1994 when it was sold. Andy was part of the team for the last few of these years, as was his wife, Susannah Hart, and believed Interbrand's story deserved to be told, by me. He said he knew bits of the story, but even these tended to be handed down anecdotes, which he knew were subject to exaggeration and distortion. Also, as he was still working in 'branding' – indeed, he is now a leading light – he was concerned about the rival claimants who said that they were the forces behind branding. He'd like to read the more reliable and accurate account – mine.

I was flattered by this interest, who wouldn't be? But I was idle too, and did nothing at first, but he persisted. Finally I dictated my account to my wife, Janet, and she typed the original manuscript some ten years ago. But then I promptly lost interest in it and deposited it in a drawer. (In truth, it also still needed a huge amount of work and I couldn't summon the energy.) Then a couple of years ago Andy ambushed me once again, and this time I responded. He also suggested the title, *Brandfather*. This at first embarrassed me, but I came to like it as ego took over.

So I must acknowledge the huge encouragement and assistance of Andy and Susannah. Also, of course, that of my wife, Janet. Many thanks!

I also must acknowledge the great help of Elen Lewis, my editor, who did much of the work involved in beating my original manuscript into shape.

My first wife, Elaine, my fellow directors at Interbrand and all my former colleagues deserve my thanks too, as do my colleagues and former colleagues at Plymouth Gin, St Peter's Brewery and Ruffians.

I have tried to tell the Interbrand story, as well as the stories of the other businesses with which I was or am still involved, as truthfully and frankly as possible, warts and all. I hope you, the reader, find my account interesting and enjoyable.

John Murphy
London, 2016

PREFACE

Everyone now knows what a brand is and the concept of branding seems to be utterly familiar to most of us, from teenagers onwards.

It is, therefore, strange to reflect that only thirty to forty years ago the word 'brand' was very little used, even in advertising, marketing and the packaged goods sectors – there were dozens of 'product managers' around but no 'brand managers' – while the word ' branding' had not even been coined.

An (some would say the) influential force behind the establishment of the concept of the brand, and of branding, in our everyday lives and in most business practice, was my former company, Interbrand. In this book, *Brandfather*, I describe how and why.

I also tell the story of the highs and lows and the successes and failures of Interbrand and of my other businesses.

Most accounts of businesses appear to me to paint a picture of steady achievement. The trajectory is reassuringly upwards, though world wars sometimes cause temporary interruptions. My experience has never been like that – success always seems to be infrequent and tenuous; failure is always just around the corner.

What's business really like? Judge for yourselves.

> *'If this business were to be split up, I would take the brands, trade marks and goodwill and you could have all the bricks and mortar – and I would fare better than you.'*
>
> John Stuart, Chairman, Quaker, 1990.

1

A RUNNING START

How my life as an entrepreneurial brand-builder was kick-started with a flat tyre and the desire to escape the bureaucracy of corporate life with a big idea about naming new products.

The story of my business life is inextricably wrapped up with the story of branding. I have built new brands from scratch, turned around the fortunes of brands that were failing, created the business that is now the world's leading brand consultancy and developed the modern techniques and tools of branding and of valuing brands that have transformed them from things that interested a few marketers, to billion-dollar assets that fascinate the world. I can even claim to have invented and first used (at least in a business context) the term 'branding', as I shall explain later.

But I am not a Richard Branson or a Bill Gates and I know that I will not be afforded even a footnote in the story of business in the twentieth century. Nor have I made the enormous fortunes of these eminent entrepreneurs, though I have made two modest fortunes and may even make a third and possibly a fourth. What I have done in my business life is have more fun and general 'sport' (i.e. mischief without malice) than most people enjoy in ten business lifetimes, or so it seems to me. Business is a fantastic game that anyone can play and where the rules are very broadly drawn; working with brands is the most fun of all – though in truth I stumbled across the value of brands almost by accident. My belief in the value and transformative power of brands did not develop overnight.

In business, you can head off in whatever direction your fancy takes you and the only thing holding you back is the reality of the marketplace – does it work commercially or not? It is a world of supreme elation and heart-stopping disappointment, of close friendships and bitter enmities, of loyalties and betrayals. The businesses I have worked in, the clients I have worked for and the colleagues I have worked with have stretched me intellectually and allowed me to participate in hundreds of projects that have covered a huge range of products and services. I have also travelled the world, stayed in many of the world's great hotels, and met interesting people from all walks of life.

My business life also seems to have taken me from one disaster to another, interspersed with occasional successes. It has been an exhilarating ride but I wouldn't have missed a minute of it. I never set out to be an entrepreneur, though from the time I was a teenager I wanted to work in business. I suppose the transition from junior businessman to junior entrepreneur is a fairly natural one, though relatively few people seem to make it. In this book I share with you my business experiences, good and bad, in the worlds of tyre marketing, consultancy, gin production, brewing and male grooming. I have tried to tell it 'as it is' or, at least, 'as I truly remember it' though I fully realise that each of us has our own individually tailored portfolio of memories.

A RUNNING START

My story begins when I joined Dunlop in 1970, aged almost twenty-six (with a degree in geography), having spent the five years since graduation in Rochdale and the US (Rhode Island and Wisconsin) with a textile and plastics machinery company called Leesona. At the time I joined, Dunlop was one of Europe's biggest companies and would soon be one of the world's biggest.

Dunlop in the early 1970s employed around 100,000 people worldwide. About half its turnover was in tyres of all kinds – for bicycles, cars, trucks, aircraft, earth movers and so on – and the rest came from a range of other broadly related rubber-based activities including the manufacture of sportswear, foam rubber products, rubber boats, fluid seals, brake systems, wheels, aircraft suspension systems, adhesives and so forth. Dunlop also had huge rubber plantations in Malaysia and, in addition to its British manufacturing operations it had major plants in the US, Canada, France, Germany, India, Pakistan, South Africa and New Zealand as well as joint ventures in Japan (with Sumitomo) and Australia (with Pacific Dunlop).

It was a vast operation and, at that time, still quite successful, but signs of impending disaster were not hard to find. Within weeks of joining, I was convinced that Dunlop would never survive, at least in its current form, but no one else seemed to share my conviction.

There were two significant incidents during my time at Dunlop that started me thinking about the potential for a brand naming business. The first was the sale of a name by Dunlop to Esso for what was, at the time, a near astronomical sum. The second, closer to home, was the problem I had in finding an international name for a new tyre. But more of these later.

My job at Dunlop was in the Corporate Planning Department. On my first day I met my new boss, a grand old man called George Slater. I was also introduced to John Simon, the joint managing director, to whom George Slater reported. In a five-minute interview on my first day John Simon told me that, as the new boy, I must keep a clear desk for a few days as matters were coming up which meant I could be useful to him. I had no idea what he was talking about, but realised that I had, in effect, been nabbed by him to become his informal personal assistant or FC, as we later came to term the role at Interbrand and as I explain later.

Towards the end of my first week, John Simon called me to his office and asked what I had been doing since I joined. I told him that I had been 'familiarising myself with the business' and mentioned the latest annual report. He asked me if I'd found anything of interest in it. In fact, I thought it was horribly tedious but I replied that I found it fascinating and that an anonymous entry in the income statements had caught my eye, an apparent windfall of £1 million, possibly £10 million or more in current terms. John Simon said he shouldn't really discuss this particular entry, but as he had had a role in 'earning' this money he would tell me the story.

NAMING OIL

In 1968 or 1969 he had received a mysterious phone call from an American law firm, requesting a meeting. Though they wouldn't state its purpose he reluctantly agreed and on the due date several senior Americans turned up in his office having all flown the Atlantic, a rarer event then than now. It transpired that a couple of them worked for Esso, the remainder were Esso's lawyers, and eventually the reason for the meeting emerged. In a few countries, including the UK and South Africa, Dunlop owned the trade mark Extron for conveyor belting and Esso wanted to buy it. Simon said he made a phone call and established that the mark was of little interest to Dunlop, but realised that for some reason it was of huge interest to Esso. He therefore asked for £1 million for the rights to the name and the price was agreed on the spot. He later realised that the purchase of the mark was an important preliminary to Esso's change of name to Exxon. For me this story was my first introduction to the potential value of a trade mark and it intrigued me.

However, the reason for my summons to John Simon's office was not to discuss trade marks, but to be briefed by him on a major development, which was due to hit the headlines within hours. In a complicated and groundbreaking arrangement, Dunlop was to merge with Pirelli of Italy to create one of the world's largest industrial companies, to be known initially (as nobody could agree on a new name) as the Dunlop-Pirelli Union. I was instructed that I was to be the 'secretariat' for the DP Union.

THE TYRE UNION

Pirelli was similar in size to Dunlop – around 100,000 employees worldwide – and, like Dunlop, derived around half of its sales from tyres. But there the similarities ended. Whereas Dunlop was strong in North America, Northern Europe, the Indian sub-continent, South Africa, Japan and Australasia, Pirelli's strength lay in Southern Europe, Turkey and South America. And whereas the non-tyre 50% of Dunlop's turnover came from a wide range of rubber-related activities, most of the remainder of Pirelli's business came from cable manufacturing, an activity unfamiliar to Dunlop.

John Simon told me that the two companies were entirely complementary as Pirelli was strong in markets where Dunlop was not, and vice versa, while Pirelli's cables business would diversify the business risk for Dunlop's shareholders. But to my mind his explanation didn't ring true.

For a start, the Italian economy at that time was in near meltdown with armed insurrection on the streets and executives of Fiat and Pirelli murdered at their desks. Spain too was an unattractive place in which to do business, because under General Franco it had sunk to second world status. And as for Greece, Turkey, Brazil and Argentina, all of them countries I had visited in the 1960s, who would want to swap assets in the US, France, Germany, UK and Japan for assets in these highly volatile markets, especially as it was nearly impossible at the time to repatriate profits, in the unlikely event one ever made any?

Dunlop, however, entered into one of the biggest ever mergers in industrial history without, I am convinced, any real thought as to the fundamentals of such an arrangement. They simply looked at the arithmetic – a company employing 200,000 people with plants in thirty countries must be better than one employing 100,000 with plants in fifteen countries. There was the unwritten assumption too, on the part of Dunlop, that Brits were superior to Italians. Even though it might be portrayed as a merger, Dunlop felt it was taking over Pirelli, and this was in the natural order of things. For its part, Pirelli was mainly interested in survival. But it was Pirelli who survived and Dunlop that collapsed.

And although I wasn't to know it at the time, watching this complex merger play out from the sidelines was a valuable business lesson for me.

RUNNING FLAT

One day in early 1970, only a week or two after the Union was announced, John Simon was visiting Tyre Technical Centre at Fort Dunlop in Birmingham and was shown a new concept developed by Tom French, a senior tyre technologist.

Only a week or two before Simon's visit, French had put some wallpaper paste into a tyre, bolted the tyre's beads to the rim using a technique developed in Formula One racing, and shown that the tyre could then run flat for many miles due to the wallpaper paste's lubrication effect and the fact that the tyre's beads were locked in position. At the time, car manufacturers such as British Leyland were keen to eliminate the spare wheel as it was expensive and took up a lot of room in their cars. French hypothesised that Dunlop could develop a run-flat tyre which would cut down accidents from tyre blow-outs, and would also avoid the need for the spare wheel, a development which would be welcomed by car manufacturers, if not by motorists.

Tom French was a charming, charismatic man with a fine war record. He also had a brilliantly inventive mind and a boundless ego. His hero was Sir Frank Whittle, inventor of the jet engine, and Tom's ambition was to be up there in the pantheon of great inventors. When John Simon and Tom French joined forces over the newly invented run-flat tyre, it was a disastrous pairing. What was in it for Simon was the opportunity to show that the Brits were top of the technical heap and inventiveness was a part of the British genius, not Italian. He liked to quote Rutherford and Whittle and conveniently forgot about Leonardo da Vinci and Marconi. He decided to hype up the run-flat tyre project as an example of Dunlop's genius and ram it down the throats of Pirelli. He believed there was no way they could exercise any sort of technical influence within the Union in the face of this invention and it would effectively seal moral and technical leadership of the vast new company for the British.

French, for his part, believed that fate had finally recognised his genius and he milked Simon's interest for all it was worth.

Within, literally, a few months of the first tentative demonstration of the run-flat tyre, Simon announced that the development was so important it was to be shown to the world. After all, car manufacturers needed to have as long a lead time as possible to develop new vehicles without a spare wheel. I was given the job of managing the run-flat tyre project and revealing it to the world.

The problem was that the supposedly fully developed new product was simply a raw invention, in fact, a very raw invention. No new tyres had been developed – we were simply using standard off the shelf tyres, the special wheels were also hand made and not suitable for mass production, the system for dispensing the lubricant within the tyres was utterly rudimentary (it was simply spooned in) and little attention had been given to service arrangements across Europe for the users of such tyres who might suffer a puncture on a Sunday night while 200 miles from home. John Simon would not, however, listen to any of the problems; he simply wished to go public and get the maximum PR, rubbing Pirelli's nose in it along the way. Tom French was a willing accomplice. I was the one who had to make it happen.

A RACING CHANCE

I was told that I had to arrange worldwide demonstrations of the new tyre for the press, car manufacturers, government bodies and safety organisations all within a two-month period – this when the product was barely invented. I negotiated a three-month extension, which brought my deadline to the end of April 1971, but this was as long as I was allowed. Given the bad weather we experienced in recent years we could not risk having the launch demonstrations in the UK and so I hired the Paul Ricard racing circuit in southern France for the purpose.

I organised a fleet of thirty cars and a mountain of wheels and tyres and despatched a team from Britain to mount the event. We booked all the hotels in Aix-en-Provence and for six weeks flew in the world's motoring press and others to view our new wonder tyre. Every working day for six weeks a chartered aircraft would land at Marseilles Airport or at the Paul Ricard airstrip. My team and I would meet our visitors, take them to their hotels and then entertain them with a fine meal. The next morning we would bring them to the racing circuit and allow them to tear around the race track while tyre side walls were blown out with small explosive charges. Everyone had a wonderful and exciting time. We would then give them a slap-up, boozy lunch and take them back to the airport.

As we waved them goodbye, the next plane would land and it would all start again. This went on for day after day and week after week. We had journalists, car designers and road safety experts from all over the world and the PR which Dunlop gained was phenomenal. The concept of driving on a flat tyre aroused, for some reason, an almost unbelievable level of interest and excitement. John Simon was beside himself. He really felt he had given the Italians one in the eye.

I was much less enthusiastic. For a start, I had never been so exhausted in my life. For our visitors it was a 24-hour party, followed in most cases by a 24-hour headache, but then it was all over. For me it was Groundhog Day. The same ghastly circus took place day after day until I could hardly stand up or think coherently. Hosting a drunken dinner for sixty people for thirty consecutive weeknights almost finished me. The final straw came when I was called from my bed at 3am by the manager of the leading hotel in Aix en Provence. Our guests on this occasion included a large Irish contingent concerned with road safety matters. One, a Roman Catholic monsignor, had insisted on bringing his assistant, a nun. After a particularly boozy evening a dozen or so of the guests, including the monsignor, remained in the bar for a lusty singsong. This did not upset the hotel manager as by then he was used to it. What concerned him was that the monsignor had wet himself quite copiously but didn't know it. He needed my advice as to whether he should ignore this or bring it to the attention of the cleric. I said to do what he liked as I was going back to bed, which I did.

A PARTY TRICK

It became clear that the other joint managing director of Dunlop, Campbell Fraser, as well as many others were hugely distrustful of John Simon's motives in jumping on the run-flat bandwagon but did not have the power or the confidence to restrain him. After all, the new tyre might just be enormously successful and might prove to be the product to knock Michelin, the clear market leader, at least in technical terms, off its perch. Secretly, too, I believe that there were few in Dunlop who minded Pirelli being second-bested, though there were also few who applauded Simon's grandstanding.

Once all the PR had died away and Simon had achieved his apparent victory over the Italians, support was slowly withdrawn from the run-flat tyre project. The project remained a Dunlop party trick ('come drive one of our cars and have a front tyre blown out at 100mph') but no real effort was made to resolve the enormous technical, production and servicing problems which needed to be overcome if the project was ever to be commercially successful. My colleague, Iain Mills, who later became the Conservative MP for Meriden and who has since sadly died, carried on bravely for some years, but nothing more was achieved other than some preliminary sales to British Leyland.

After my stint on the run-flat tyre project I was put to work at Fort Dunlop where I was concerned with UK tyre marketing, a role that did not really suit me. However, I continued as secretary to the DP Union and its goings-on. For a start, Birmingham in the 1970s was not what one might call a 'happening' place. Nor was I very much interested in tyres, cars or motoring. I had some great colleagues and some good times (Murray Walker, who later became a well known motor-racing commentator, handled the Dunlop account on behalf of Masius, the advertising agency, and was great fun) but all the time I was acutely aware of the storm clouds gathering over Dunlop and had no wish to be there when the company finally collapsed. It would look pretty bad on my CV.

The final straw came when I was taken aside by John Simon. He had miraculously survived in his job, though Campbell Fraser was clearly the senior of the two joint MD's. He told me that the company had great plans for me and I could expect to be on the main board within two or three years, by around the age of thirty. He said that Dunlop would like meanwhile for me to gain some senior line experience and he proposed that I be appointed as sales or marketing director at one of the major subsidiaries, probably Dunlop India or Dunlop Canada, for two to three years. All being well I would then return to the UK and join the main board.

This prospect filled me with horror. The salary would probably have been quite good and a chauffeured limo and a place in the directors' dining room would have been nice perks but, by my reckoning, I would reach the main board round about the time that the company imploded so that Dunlop's problems would become my problems. Nor, of course, was I too keen to spend more time abroad, as much as I liked India and Canada. I immediately started to think in earnest about getting out and starting a business of my own. But what could I do?

'MAY THE BLUEBIRD OF HAPPINESS HOVER OVER YOUR RUBBER FACTORY...'

And, quite by chance, the run-flat tyre project gave me my big idea. This project was still limping along and it still reported to me, though I now had other, wider responsibilities. For two or three years it had been referred to simply as 'the run-flat project' or 'the total mobility project', a name coined by Iain Mills when he joined me as its day-to-day manager. Though at the time I knew nothing about branding (indeed 'branding' as such didn't exist then), I realised that we ought to give the new product a proprietary name so that people came to know it by our name and not by a generic description. The engineers and marketing people proposed dozens of potential names but these all proved to be unsuitable, inherently unprotectable or already registered by others. Masius, our ad agency, also proposed dozens of 'names' but these were even worse. Most were in fact slogans, rather than protectable names, and, for the first time, I realised that ad agencies, though they might know something about advertising, knew little about branding or marketing.

John Simon then got in on the act. In my absence, on an extended business trip, he telexed (we didn't have faxes or emails in those days) all the

Dunlop businesses worldwide, inviting them to participate in an employee competition to name the run-flat tyre. He said all entries should be sent to me. When I returned from my trip to Detroit to visit Ford my desk was completely covered in mail from around the world. When I confronted John Simon about this, he said I had abjectly failed to name the new tyre so he was taking matters out of my hands. I ploughed through thousands of entries and came to realise that amateur naming was not the route to go. Dunlop's East African employees all seemed to favour names with overt macho, sexual connotations, which referred to the potency and vigour of the Dunlop tyre company. The Brits, on the other hand, liked punning names such as 'Jack the Gripper' and 'Dunlophlat' (John Simon's personal favourite), whilst the favoured Japanese entry was a name which, when translated from the Japanese, apparently meant 'may the bluebird of happiness hover over your rubber factory'.

I can remember sending bottles of champagne to employees around the world as 'runners up' prizes, while announcing that we still hadn't found the name we wanted. Then a colleague, Keith Pybus, told me that he had read a piece in the *Financial Times* about a company just set up in Paris called Novamark which specialised in thinking up brand names. I gave them the job of naming the new tyre and they came up with the name Denovo.

John Simon was not too keen on the name Denovo, preferring Dunlophlat, and only abandoned his favourite when I told him that he could not be serious. The reason for the urgency to find a name was that we were just about to start manufacturing the first production run-flat tyres for British Leyland to offer as an option on the Mini and we needed to engrave the name into the sidewall of the tyres. Cars fitted with Dunlop's run-flat tyres were to be shown at the Motor Show in a few weeks' time and an instant decision on the name was needed. Reluctantly John Simon agreed that we could adopt the name Denovo but he said he needed final authorisation from the main board.

I replied that surely the main board would not concern itself with such a trivial decision as a product name. He assured me there was no way he could make such an important decision without main board approval. However, an extraordinary board meeting was being held that same afternoon and he would phone me later to let me know if the proposed name had been approved.

Late that afternoon he called to say I had my name – Denovo – and could go ahead with engraving the tyre moulds. He then expanded on how the decision had been taken. He told me that the Dunlop Pirelli Union, which was still nominally in existence, was proving so disastrous that Dunlop was having to write down its huge investment in Pirelli to zero. The extraordinary board meeting had been called to approve a write-off of hundreds of millions of pounds, possibly £5 billion or so at current values. He told me that the special board meeting had lasted for two hours and that the board had taken five minutes to write off the hundreds of millions and one hour and fifty-five minutes to approve the choice of the name Denovo.

My business idea was born.

2

STARTING UP ON MY OWN

In which I started the first brand naming business in the UK and began to wonder if anybody would buy this curious service I was offering.

Starting up my own business was more about frustration with Dunlop and with major British companies in general, than about any desperation to run my own show. I simply wanted to be able to make my own mistakes. I also had a sneaky feeling that I wasn't really cut out for the corporate life. Minding my 'ps and qs' and toeing the party line was not my style.

For a year or so before I left Dunlop I ruminated about what sort of business I might set up. I had very limited capital, though my wife was by this time a junior doctor in the National Health Service (NHS) and, at a pinch, her salary could feed us both, at least for a while. The problem I faced was that all my business experience was in big businesses. Had my father owned a newsagent's shop (in fact, he was a toolmaker on the shop floor of Ford Motor Co. in Dagenham) or had I worked in a theatrical agency I could possibly have set up a similar business; as it was I was stumped for a big idea which was within my limited resources.

Then a friend, Malcolm Ridley, who had worked with me at Dunlop, called to say that his new employer, Noble Lowndes, part of the Hill Samuel merchant bank, was looking for a marketing director for one of its companies. I must confess that the world of financial services had never held much appeal, but I was well aware that the rewards in this sector were (and still are) disproportionately large. I had always believed that people who made things were pursuing an honourable course in life, whereas those who shuffled money or played the markets or sold pension plans produced nothing of real value. In spite of this, financial reality overtook me. I successfully applied for the job and moved back to London.

My reservations about my suitability proved correct. Though Noble Lowndes turned out to be generous employers and I came to realise that the services they offered could be valuable; working in financial services wasn't for me. I might, even so, have lacked the courage to escape had not the Chancellor, in his Spring Budget of 1974, made tax changes which meant that the market for our financial services was much reduced and the need for people like me reduced too. I therefore resolved to think once again about how I might start up on my own.

BAD TIMING

The omens were not encouraging. Harold Wilson and Edward Heath, as Prime Ministers, both seemed determined to wreck the British economy and union leaders like Red Robbo at Austin Rover seemed fixed on destroying what remained of British industry. It was an appalling time. The 1960s had proved exciting with the Beatles, the Rolling Stones, Mary Quant, Biba and Carnaby Street, but the 1970s were miserable. We produced horrid cars, which nobody wanted and which kept breaking down, our ship building industry had virtually disappeared, a new industrial dispute broke out every week and the government seemed powerless. I really wished I'd stayed in the US, where I had worked in the late 1960s, but realised that I had to make the most of my decision to return to the UK. I wanted to start my own business but knew my timing was appalling.

Having worked at Noble Lowndes it was clear that the answer probably lay in some sort of service business. I could start such a business without much capital and as for marketing my services, I had seen the power of PR in operation at Dunlop. I started to think about setting up a service business where my main route to market would be heavy PR, but what should it be?

A FRENCH PARTNERSHIP

Luckily I had maintained contact with Novamark, the small naming company in Paris which I had employed to develop the name Denovo for Dunlop's run-flat tyre. Jean-Yves Fournis, president of the company, was a good chap who phoned me up from time to time for help with various problems. In particular, if he wanted to check out the suitability in English of a name he was developing for a French client, he would ask for an 'off the cuff' opinion. We occasionally met in London for a night out together. In early 1974 he contacted me to say that Novamark wanted to start an operation in London. Would I be interested? They had no funds to invest and no British clients but perhaps we could work together? I was intrigued.

At the time British companies were looking at European markets much more seriously as a result of Britain's decision to join the Common Market. In the past, British products had mainly been marketed in the home market and in former Empire countries. But times were changing and businesses now needed suitable and protectable names throughout Europe and the rest of the world and not just in English-speaking countries, or so I believed.

I had also been struck, while working on the run-flat tyre project, by how difficult it is to find a name that is acceptable and protectable internationally. Even by the early 1970s the world's trade mark registers were crowded. Long before the advent of the Internet and improved international communications, brand owners were concerned that their new names should not cause offence or derision in overseas markets. Accordingly, I felt that there might be an opportunity for a name creation business in London.

I negotiated a deal with Novamark Paris whereby I would open a Novamark business in London, funding it in its entirety. I would have a majority of the equity and Novamark Paris would hold a minority. I would also have exclusive rights to the Novamark concept and service in English-speaking markets. In other markets we would, if the opportunity arose, work together on a co-operative basis.

I was happy with this arrangement and liked my new partners in Paris, even though I knew that these new colleagues did not own that business. In fact, it was owned by two mysterious brothers who seemed to avoid any opportunity to meet me. The main asset that the French company gave me was credibility, as it would have been difficult to start a name creation business from scratch without any track record or examples of our work, or so I believed. I suspected, however, that name creation was something for which I had an aptitude, so had no great reservations about my ability to satisfy clients, should I ever be successful in winning any.

The major problem I encountered of a 'product' nature was that Novamark Paris did not have a strong methodology for name creation. When they had worked for me on the Denovo project they had achieved a result, but I was not impressed with how they went about things. It all looked somewhat haphazard. Had we not been up against a really tight deadline, which meant that we more or less had to accept whatever the process produced, I doubt that I would have been altogether happy with the name they proposed for the new tyre and would have insisted that the process was repeated. (In fact, I probably would have been wrong had I done so, because, over time, I came to recognise that Denovo was a much better solution than I gave it credit for initially. It was only the product itself that was faulty.)

In the first half of 1974 I spent much of my spare time reading marketing textbooks to familiarise myself with creative and market research techniques. I then put together what I considered to be a strong name creation methodology. Indeed, I know that the procedures I developed then are still used widely today by the entire name creation industry, one which is now quite large.

A ROOM OF ONE'S OWN

I also had to solve the problem of office accommodation. I needed, or so I thought, a prestige address but I certainly couldn't afford flashy offices. My plan was to operate from the spare room of our flat: when my wife and I had returned to London from Birmingham, me to work for Noble Lowndes and she to take up a position at a London hospital, we found it impossible to sell our curious house in the centre of Warwick. We therefore decided to rent a flat in the new Barbican Centre on the edge of the City of London. Our spare bedroom was designated as my new office. But it was not possible to use our address for business mail or as a registered office as this contravened the terms of our lease. I therefore took a poste restante address on Baker Street and, for the first year or so, every working day would begin with a trip on the Circle Line from Barbican to Baker Street to collect my mail.

In September 1974, having resigned my job with Noble Lowndes, negotiated a partnership arrangement with Novamark Paris, formed a new company in London, equipped our spare bedroom with a desk and rudimentary office equipment, taken an accommodation address in Baker Street, developed some basic methodologies and taken out a second mortgage on our new country house in the Cotswolds, I was ready to start.

All I needed were clients. Would anybody ever buy this curious service I was offering? After all, the only company in the world offering a dedicated name creation service, as far as I could tell, was Novamark Paris and I doubted they were booming. Certainly, I would be the first in the UK and probably in the entire English-speaking world.

3

A NOTE TO LORD DARTMOUTH

*In which I learnt how to deal with an almost complete lack
of interest in my service, but succeeded in naming a business
for Sainsbury's: Homebase.*

When I first told people I was starting a naming business it was clear that
almost everyone thought I was quite mad. Who, they asked, would be crazy
enough to pay money for a name when in a few moments they could think
up one for themselves for nothing? Almost no one I talked to believed I had
the slightest chance of success, which made me even more determined to
prove them wrong. Moreover, in the early 1970s there seemed to be great
hostility in Britain towards anything or anyone entrepreneurial. Among
large sectors of the population even working in business was considered
grubby: 'honourable' people worked for the Civil Service or the NHS.

We had, earlier, sold our house in Warwick and bought a country house
in the Cotswolds as our flat in London was leasehold but we wished to
remain in the property market. An elderly woman neighbour who lived in
a grand Georgian mansion near our new country pile invited us to dinner.
It was kind of her to do so and I tried to be on my best behaviour admiring
her furniture and beautiful possessions. In particular I commented on her
exquisite embroidered curtains. The windows they decorated must have
been twelve feet high and there were six of them in the dining room. She
said, rather grandly, that one of her ancestors had been involved in the
sacking of the old Summer Palace in Peking in 1860, and had taken the
curtains home as booty. They had been in the family ever since. A little later
in the evening, as conversation developed, she turned to me and asked me
what I did for a living. I told her I was just starting a small business and she
immediately lost interest, saying, "So you're in trade?" By then I'd had a few
glasses of wine and, for sport, replied, "Yes, but I buy my own curtains."

Fortunately, I don't think she heard me, but it was clear that in her view and that of many others 'trade' was disreputable.

A LEGAL TRADE

The only person I can remember, apart from my wife and my new associates in Paris, who supported the idea of starting a name creation business in London was my former colleague, Mike Grant, the head of trade marks at Dunlop. Before joining Dunlop, Mike had worked in private practice in London and New York and believed there was a growing need among businesses for a professional, competent name creation service. When I told him that I was going to set up on my own, he very much wished to join me.

His proposal was that he would handle all the legal searches and clearances required when developing a new trade mark; he also said that he had friends and contacts in London and New York whom he thought would send him trade mark legal work if he were to leave Dunlop. The problem he had was that he could not afford to take any financial risks. He worked at Fort Dunlop in Birmingham and lived near Burton-on-Trent with his wife and family. He needed the security of a continuing income and certainly could not move to London until the company was established. I liked Mike and felt he would make a good partner so I agreed that I would start the business on my own but, as and when he was able to join me, I would give him a stake in the business without his having to make any investment. Meanwhile, he agreed that he would be available at the end of the phone should I ever need help.

The first thing I did once I had started the business was to draft a four-page leaflet and, what I thought to be, a punchy covering letter. I had these printed and felt they looked pretty damned good. I also spent weeks of my life poring over directories and reference books in order to put together a comprehensive mailing list of key marketing executives in British and Irish consumer products businesses. My sister, Eileen, typed the names and addresses on to adhesive labels in the evenings and eventually I had a mailing list of some 7,000 names.

'SATISFACTION OR YOUR BLOCKAGE BACK.'

One issue I wrestled with was how I should charge for our services. The obvious solution was to charge on the basis of time plus disbursements, but I didn't think that clients would welcome this approach – it is always disconcerting to give a brief to a lawyer or consultant and to know that the meter is running but not what the final bill will be. Nor did I think that I would much like this approach, as I was pretty sure I would make a good fist of creating international brand names and would be able to turn 'em out efficiently and expeditiously. I suspected that time plus disbursements wouldn't make me much of a living.

I therefore decided to draw up a scale of fees based upon what I thought the problem was worth, not how long it took me to solve it. I reckoned that the average new product launch in the UK at that time cost perhaps one third to half a million pounds, most of which would be spent on the first year's advertising. If I charged a fixed fee of, say, £5,000 or so to develop an attractive, memorable, available and protectable UK name for the new product, which the owner could use for decades, then it was a bargain, or so I thought. And if I could do so in ten minutes with only a few disbursements, so what? My client got exactly what he wanted and knew the precise cost in advance. There would be no extras and I would guarantee to continue working until the problem was solved. At the time Dyno-Rod, the drain clearance people, had an advertisement on the London Underground where they guaranteed 'satisfaction or your blockage back'. That appealed to me and I quoted it to clients for years as the basis for our fees.

Eventually – by the 1980s – our price list ran from £10,000 for a UK product or service name to £200,000 or more for a name usable and protectable in all the main countries of the world. For the agreed fee we would prepare a positioning study, create names, agree a shortlist in conjunction with the client, conduct full language checks and consumer preference checks, and undertake all legal searches and clearances. Such clearances were particularly important, as well as tedious and time-consuming, as a name is useless unless it is legally available.

At the time I sent out my first mailshot to the 7,000 lucky recipients, much of this lay in the future. I can remember my sense of anticipation when waiting for a response to my mailshots, any response. In fact I only had one, and I was enormously grateful for it. It was from Aspro-Nicholas, then based in Slough in the office block where the BBC TV comedy series *The Office* was later filmed. Aspro-Nicholas gave me the job developing a UK name for a new over-the-counter medicine. I could not have been happier. I had been in business less than three months and had my first client.

OFF THE RECORD

But I almost stumbled at the first hurdle and in doing so learned a lesson that has stayed with me ever since. It was about dealing with the press. When I started Novamark I had phoned a number of business newspapers and magazines and sent out lots of press releases. The trade magazines gave me some short mentions, mainly vaguely mocking, but none of the nationals showed any interest. Then, about the time I won my first job from Aspro-Nicholas, a journalist from the *Financial Times* phoned me to say he would like to do an interview. I met him in my Barbican flat; not telling him it was also my office. I told him the story of Novamark, why trade marks were so important, why they were the only aspect of a product that was never changed, how they were the key to successful international marketing, how they were the central component of the intellectual property owned by many companies and so forth. He showed great interest and, getting into my stride, I asked him if I could tell him a story, off the record, which had just been recounted to me by a client. He agreed to this and I told him about a major naming problem Aspro-Nicholas had encountered in Australia, which cost them a fortune to resolve. They had told me this story a few days earlier, though not, fortunately, in confidence. It was also fortunate that the story had been widely reported in the Australian press, though I did not know this at the time.

A couple of days later I bought the *Financial Times* and there was the piece on Novamark with a nice picture of me. I read it and my heart nearly stopped: in the article the Aspro-Nicholas story was recounted in detail. I had not realised that 'off the record' is often interpreted as meaning that the story can be re-told but not attributed. I thought it meant that a journalist could be given such information for the purposes of background briefing, but would not publish any information provided in this way. How wrong I was. I made humble apologies to Aspro-Nicholas but luckily they did not take offence. I think they realised how green I was. One of their team later told me that he had made a hash of PR matters himself on a couple of occasions and knew how easy this was to do. I was forgiven but knew it was a lucky miss.

FEELING AT HOME WITH SAINSBURY'S

Over the course of the next few months my business followed a set pattern – lots of mailshots and as much PR as I could get. In particular, I was concerned not so much with selling my services as establishing the principle that companies ought to take naming seriously. From time to time I was even lucky enough to win a new assignment. One of these early jobs was for Sainsbury's. They were planning to go into the DIY business in partnership with a major Belgian retailer. I won the job of naming the new venture as none of the candidate names they had considered, which had been developed in-house and by their advertising agency, had turned out to be legally available. Time was running short. My client was Peter Davis, their managing director, and we got on well together though he clearly thought that what I was doing was completely barmy. He said that all Sainsbury's wanted was a company name. They did not wish us to conduct any trade mark searches as the name would not be used as a trade mark on products. I said that whether or not the new name was used on products, we had to search the trade marks register as they could not use a company name that was in conflict with a product brand name used in the same business area. Besides which, company names in the retail sector are particularly likely to soon be used on products as they were bound to develop private label products. They should be prepared for this.

Eventually it was reluctantly agreed that the new name should be both a corporate name and a trade mark covering all the goods likely to be sold in the new stores. When I checked these out, I realised that Sainsbury's needed a name that was available and protectable in over twenty different trade mark classes. What had started out as a relatively simple job turned out to be a massive legal searching exercise. Fortunately, by this time, Mike Grant had thrown in his job at Dunlop and joined me in London so we had the expertise in-house to handle this complex assignment. Homebase was the name that was finally selected (I am proud to say that I championed it quite hard) and I know it worked extremely well. Interestingly, the name,

Homebase, was used as both a company name and as a brand name on scores of own-label products.

Indeed, Sainsbury's liked our handling of the legal searches so much they handed us all their trade mark legal work. Similarly, the newly formed British Telecom, which was spun off from the Post Office, for whom we conducted a name creation assignment, also gave us all their trade mark legal work on completion of the job. Within a couple of years or so we had the makings of a name creation business with a new assignment every couple of months as well as an embryonic trade mark legal practice (we called it Grant & Co for obvious reasons) which conducted our legal searches and also handled trade mark filings and other related trade mark legal work for clients. Such ongoing clients instructed Grant & Co direct once the naming assignment had been completed.

The arcane science of clearing a name legally on an international basis is little understood, even by many trade mark lawyers. The normal way of clearing a shortlist of, say, a dozen names in a dozen countries is to search all the names in all countries simultaneously, a process which can be extremely expensive. In practice, however, if one finds a problem with one of the names in one important market, say the UK, it is reasonably likely that the same problem exists in all twelve countries. It makes sense, therefore (or at least it made sense at the time; the new European trade mark regime has changed the game, as have databases and computerised search techniques), to search all dozen names in one major country, the survivors in the second country and so on. With experience, the apparently enormous cost of the trade mark searches could be kept under control such that our margins could be maintained.

Mike Grant was kept fairly busy conducting our legal searches, but the sporadic name creation assignments we won were not enough to keep me out of mischief, and there was much amusement to be had along the way. One day, for example, I was phoned up by a nice lady who said that our mailshot had arrived on her desk.

"Do you really want me to put it in front of my boss, Lord Dartmouth?" she asked.

"Yes," I replied, "Why not?"

"Because you've addressed him as Lord Fartmouth."

She sent the letter back to me and I re-addressed it.

4

FROM CARPETS TO CARS

*In which a sheer piece of good luck launched my brand
naming business for good and I named the Metro for Austin
Rover.*

I quickly came to realise that starting a new business in a new field can be much harder than starting a new business in an established field. This is because one needs to establish a market before selling one's proprietary products or services into it, whereas with a new product or service in an established field, it's 'simply' about grabbing business from competitors. Setting up an entirely new business service is a long slog and requires tremendous amounts of patience, something that I don't possess in large quantities.

I had been used to being kept busy and found the long periods of relative inactivity in my new business waiting for new assignments quite wearing. Fortunately my old employer, Noble Lowndes, came to the rescue. They needed help with the preparation of a strategic plan for their business but had not been impressed with the various consultants who had pitched for the work. So they invited me to pitch and I landed a substantial consultancy contract from them, which kept me busy for months.

This income was invaluable because we were struggling financially. Upon the arrival of Mike Grant we had taken a small suite of offices on Bond Street and the cost of these, plus our mailshots, a secretary, Mike Grant's salary and other overheads was considerable. Indeed, even with the consultancy and other income, the company took over five years to become profitable and I was not able to draw a salary from the business for a few more years thereafter. My wife's salary from the NHS and, later, my income from consultancy had to stretch to cover us.

Noble Lowndes later recommended me as a strategy consultant to a number of their clients including Queensway Discount Warehouses of

Norwich, a major furniture and carpet chain. I met one of the directors of Queensway in London. He was interested in hiring me and asked that I go to Norwich early the next week to meet Gerry Parish, the owner of the company and the rest of the Queensway Board.

CARPET WARS

The following Monday I was met on arrival in the lobby of Queensway's head office by Gerry Parish's secretary. She took me to Gerry's office and said his desk had been cleared and I was to use it. She told me that there had been a blazing row earlier that morning among the directors (it was nothing to do with me, however) and three had resigned. Gerry himself had gone home and said he wouldn't be coming back. He had told her that the new consultant coming up from London that day (that is, me) was now in charge. I was to run the business; it was now my show!

I was dumbfounded. I had never met Gerry Parish. I knew nothing about retailing or about the discount furniture and carpet business. No fee had been agreed. Nothing. And Queensway was not a small operation. It had, at the time, over thirty-five large out-of-town warehouses around the country from Exeter to Edinburgh and employed over 700 people.

My initial instinct was to get on the train back to London, but I sensed that I might enjoy the challenge of managing this curious business. We also needed the consultancy fees. And Queensway desperately needed help, even my unskilled help.

I ran Queensway as managing director for the next two years, though it was agreed that I could disappear for the occasional day or so on Novamark's business. I also agreed an appropriate salary with Queensway. Half of this I took personally, and the other half was paid to Novamark as compensation for the loss of my day-to-day services. It was this regular income that paid Mike Grant's salary and allowed the company to survive those early lean years.

Running Queensway turned out to be hugely exciting and great fun. Retailing is a form of street trading and it appealed to the Essex 'barrow boy' in me. We got the company's finances under control, restructured the board and over the course of the next eighteen months opened a dozen or so new stores in locations such as South West London, Birmingham, Sunderland, Paisley and Aberdeen. I found it all thoroughly exhilarating!

I also learned about buying and selling businesses – this was my first introduction to the process. It transpired that Gerry Parish was keen to sell the company as quickly as possible, but I quickly came to realise that many of those who showed an interest in buying it either didn't have the wherewithal to conclude a deal or thought that Gerry Parish, an uncomplicated and straightforward man, could be taken for a ride.

Eventually we were approached by Phil Harris of Harris Carpets, now Lord Harris. It was, by this time, clear that we would have to bow to the inevitable as there was no way that Queensway could remain independent, given Gerry's determination to sell. Neither I nor the other executive directors felt there was any choice. Accordingly, we sold up and I was shown the door. I returned then to Novamark, a business that had, in effect, been on hold for the previous two years.

LADY LUCK

Much is written in business books and taught at business schools about strategies, 'prime mover' status, opportunity models and similar guff. My experience is that success as an entrepreneur comes from hard work, self-belief, bloody-minded determination and huge slices of the most valuable commodity in business: luck.

When I returned to Novamark, luck was on my side. One day, soon after my return, I received a call from Terry Nolan, a senior marketing executive at Austin Rover, formerly British Leyland. He asked that I come to Longbridge urgently as he had a problem that he wished to discuss. I met him that afternoon and it turned out that his 'problem' was finding a name for the company's important new car, designated as the successor to the hugely popular Mini. This potential new assignment was, accordingly, one of the most high-profile UK jobs one could possibly wish for.

By the late 1970s, there were the first stirrings of renewed business confidence in the UK and the nation's hopes for industrial and business survival seemed to hang around two huge, high-profile projects: the Anglo-French Concorde supersonic passenger jet project and the new car being developed by Austin Rover. Indeed, these two projects were, at the time, the most expensive industrial undertakings in British history and the level of public interest and anxiety they generated is difficult now to believe. The newsreels told tales of the robots being installed to build the new car at the huge Austin Rover plant outside Birmingham and of the ability of the new car to save the jobs of hundreds of thousands of workers. It would even restore Britain's faith in itself as an industrial nation. To be given the job of naming this new car, as we were, was an unbelievable coup for Novamark.

It transpired that the new car, which a few months later was to be known as the Metro, was originally planned as a successor to the Mini and was to have been called the Mini or perhaps the Mini 2. However, sales of the old Mini continued to be quite strong and the company realised it would have to continue producing the Mini alongside the new car for some time, as it could not afford to discontinue production of this model; hence the need for a new name for the planned car. Terry Nolan told me at the time of our meeting that the company had been trying to find such a name for the previous two years, but whenever they chose a new name, it proved to be unavailable or unsuitable in one or other important market. As the new car was to be sold around the world, or so they hoped, the name had to be appropriate and available in all major markets. Terry told me that the job of finding the new name had become a nightmare and Austin Rover was now in a serious fix as pre-production models simply had a blank plate on the boot lid where the name should be. He told me, too, that virtually all the sales literature had been designed and television ads had been shot, but all were missing the name. They were desperate; we must succeed and we must do so very soon.

I told him we could do the job and do it well and quoted a price; it was agreed on the spot. Before I left his office he gave me a ring binder containing the thousands of names developed internally, by Saatchi & Saatchi and by other advisers, all of which had been considered and rejected for various reasons. I was elated at winning the assignment but deeply worried as to whether we could truly succeed, particularly when so many thousands of names had already been rejected and we were under the tightest possible time constraints. I should also tell you that Novamark, the 'we' to whom I refer, was, at the time, a team of just three: Mike Grant, Eileen Chandler (my sister, who was our secretary), and me.

A CAR BY ANY OTHER NAME…

I travelled back to London, both elated and scared. If we succeeded in naming the new car we would, I knew, be made. But how on earth could we satisfy the company when it clearly had no idea at all what it was looking for?

I decided that the first thing I must do was create a naming strategy and get the company's agreement to it. Fortunately, I had noticed in the past, when running creativity groups on other assignments, that consumers liked to see some form of symmetry and rationale in the naming systems used by car companies. I had also been struck by how 'involved' consumers could be with product names and 'designators' (i.e. numbers and initials), particularly with the names of their motor cars or motorcycles. I remember one consumer saying that he disliked the system used at that time by Fiat (127, 128, 131, 132 etc.) because the higher numbers did not necessarily denote bigger and more expensive cars, as they should do. On the other hand, everyone seemed to applaud the systems used by Mercedes and BMW, as they perceived an underlying logic in the system. By contrast, Austin Rover's naming was all over the place: there was no underlying rationale and names, numbers and initials seemed to be used at random.

I therefore proposed to Austin Rover that they adopt a naming system for the new car and all subsequent cars in the range whereby the first letter in every case would be an 'M' and as the cars became larger and more expensive, the M-prefix names would become longer and lusher. The existing Mini would be the smallest car in the range and was the reason for the choice of M-names, so the new car's name had to start with this letter. Within a few days, this naming proposal was accepted and from then on the job was relatively straightforward.

As usual we used consumer groups (talented volunteers to whom we paid a small fee) as well as a lot of desk research to produce shortlists of names, which we checked for language suitability and 'fit'. Mike Grant then conducted initial legal searches on the survivors. Finally we arrived at a working list of about thirty names, all starting with M, which we presented to Austin Rover. I can remember that they liked virtually all of them but they particularly favoured about a dozen names and we were told to get on with checking and clearing as many of these names as quickly as possible, so they could have a reasonably large field from which to choose. We had about six weeks to do this, but Christmas lay slap in the middle. I recall spending part of Christmas week trailing around the offices of obscure airlines in London (Syrian Airlines, Air Cameroon, Iran Air and so forth) tracking down native speakers to ensure the selected names were not offensive in Farsi or other such languages. We also conducted consumer-ranking exercises in key markets to determine consumer preferences. At the same time, we were extending the legal searches into far-flung countries. We were well into the process and it was going well.

A FAMILY NAME

Then, a bombshell. Shortly after Christmas, just when we could see a conclusion to the project, I received a phone call early one morning from Sir Michael Edwardes, the South African boss of Austin Rover and perhaps the highest profile businessman in Britain at that time. He was a man who saw his entire glittering career as hinging on the success of the new car. He told me that while he and his family had been flying back from South Africa after Christmas they had indulged in a bit of name creation on the upper deck of their Boeing 747 and had come up with the new name. We were therefore to stop work forthwith on the names we had developed ("Drop everything immediately" – he could be extremely imperious) and put all our efforts into clearing the name he, his wife and his kids had come up with. I asked him what this was and he said it was 'Mate'. He elaborated that it fitted the agreed naming strategy and it was chirpy and friendly. He asked me what I thought and I said I believed at first sight that it was fine but as we were so far advanced on clearing the other names, all of which were equally strong, it seemed a shame to go back to the beginning of the process and lose so much time. He responded that I was to do as I was told and slammed the phone down.

We did of course do as we were told and immediately restarted the entire process of checks and legal clearances on his proposed name, Mate. However, the following morning, at the same time, I received a further call from Sir Michael. He told me that I was to forget about Mate and go back to the other names; he'd changed his mind. I said that was fine but asked him the reason for this. He said he'd looked up the work 'mate' in the dictionary and one of the meanings of 'mate', or more correctly 'maté', is a stimulating caffeine drink made from the leaf of a South American tree. He said that under the circumstances 'mate' was clearly an entirely unsuitable name for his new car – he couldn't use a name that was also that of a herbal tea. I replied that I had also looked up the verb 'to mate' in the dictionary and 'to mate' means 'to copulate'. Why was he so worried about herbal tea when he didn't care about references to copulation? He told me not to be impertinent and slammed down the phone on me once again. We were back to the original shortlist. But Sir Michael had another trick up his sleeve, which was later to cause us even more sleepless nights.

As we continued to work on the shortlist of names, we slowly shaved away the many problems that emerged in our searches of the world's trade mark registers. Clearly, we could not risk a high-profile launch and then have a third party claim that 'you have stolen my name', even if such a claim was totally without foundation (owners of names can have curious ideas as to the extent of their rights). We had to deal in advance with all potential problems, even those that might not, in the longer term, prove to be valid. We were, however, making excellent progress and were slap on target.

Then one morning I got an urgent telephone call from Terry Nolan. He told me that Austin Rover now required three names, not just one and that all three needed to be cleared for use worldwide. It transpired that Sir Michael had been speaking at a dinner the previous night at which the Prince of Wales, also a speaker, had criticised British management for not consulting with its workers on key issues. Sir Michael announced, off the cuff, that no one could accuse him of not consulting the workers. Austin Rover's workers were not only consulted on all important matters, they were even to make the final choice of name for the new car!

Clearly, our new shortlist should now contain several names, not just one. We therefore had more frantic work to do, fortunately within weeks, we had cleared three names on a worldwide basis: Metro, Maestro and Match.

Our legal searches necessarily covered vehicles and all the many components and services relating to vehicles – tyres, seating, engines, insurance services, maintenance, the lot. Austin Rover hired the Electoral Reform Society to conduct a poll of employees in order to choose a name from our shortlist and Metro came out on top. One of the ballot papers choosing the name Metro was pulled out of the hat and the lucky employee received the first Metro off the production line.

When the name of the new car was made public, it was the lead item on the BBC TV evening news and received fantastic coverage elsewhere. With the agreement of Austin Rover ("But if Michael Edwardes says anything, don't tell him we said you could do it"), I called up the *Sunday Times* and asked them if they would like the exclusive story on the naming of the new car. They not only liked it, they decided it was such a hot story they ran it as a major feature in their colour magazine. We had suddenly hit the big time. Business really picked up from then on. We had become one of the best-known and most talked about small businesses in Britain.

5

A HORSE CALLED STARION

In which a series of hiccups forced me to focus all my efforts
on the naming business.

I loved working in the name creation business. Every time I was asked to quote for a new job I was introduced to a secret new product as well as to a company's hopes and plans. It was like being a business voyeur. I found that new product development takes a great deal of the attention and energy of consumer products businesses and that some of the company's brightest people work in this area. And not only that – every single assignment was different from the last. I might be simultaneously involved in naming a new drug, a new soft drink, a new car, a new condom and a new company. Every project introduced me to new people, a new market and a new challenge.

With some projects the problem was mainly strategic – the company simply didn't know what sort of name it wanted for its new product but once we had proposed a personality for the new product, whether that might be technical/scientific, feminine, Italian, childlike or so on, it would all fall into place.

In other cases the problem might be to find a name that was linguistically acceptable in forty or fifty markets so we spent our whole time checking names with native speakers and poring over a vast matrix of possibilities. Other times legal searches and negotiations seemed to play the major part. We'd clear the preferred name or names in a dozen key countries and would then come unstuck in Portugal or Turkey and have to start all over again.

I loved the blend of creativity, strategy, research and law. I also loved the prospect that any phone call might turn out to be a new project in a whole new sector with a whole new set of problems. It reminded me of when I was an undergraduate in the early 1960s hitchhiking from Boston to Vancouver, down to Los Angeles and back to New York along Route 66. Any car or truck pulling up meant a new adventure and every ride took me to a new destination.

I also enjoyed the 'sport'. I could never take the name creation business or myself too seriously. By sheer good luck I had stumbled on one of the most entertaining activities I could possibly be involved in and I considered myself massively fortunate. I wasn't going to spoil it by pretending it was a serious business.

A HORSE CALLED STARION

I had good business reasons, too, for creating mischief. I needed to make companies take their names and trade marks seriously. One way of doing this was to broadcast as widely as I could the many naming cock-ups that companies had made in the past so that they would be more careful in the future and would realise that they needed specialist help, preferably from me. Many of the naming horror stories still in circulation – for example, that Rolls Royce almost called a new car the Silver Mist, not realising that 'Mist' can mean 'crap' in German – were given plenty of airtime by me.

I also remember the morning a Dutch client, the principal of a major car importing business, phoned me from the Tokyo Motor Show. He told me that he had a fabulous story for me and I should get lots of publicity from it. He said he knew it would appeal to me, and it did. He told me he was on his company's stand at the show as he spoke and that next door was the stand of Mitsubishi Motors. They had unveiled that day an exotic, expensive sports car called the Starion. He said he had been on to Mitsubishi's stand and asked why they had chosen the name Starion for their lovely new car. They said that they already produced a car called the Colt and had chosen Starion for the new car because this car was larger and more powerful than the Colt. "You know what a starion is?" they said to him, "It's a f*****g horse." He replied, "No, in English, the word is stallion, not starion." They said, "Yes, starion." "No, stallion." "Yes, starion." Eventually the penny dropped but it took a long time. He went on to help them, in their panic, draw up a press release claiming that the name Starion was a contraction of the two words 'star' and 'orion'. I phoned up the *Times Business Diary* that morning and told them the story and it was in the press the next morning and repeated later by many journals and on TV and radio. The Today programme on

BBC Radio 4 had particular fun with it and the story earned a great deal of publicity for names and the importance of getting them right. It also paved the way to the opening of our new office in Tokyo, as Japanese companies became particularly sensitive to the 'problem' of bad product names.

THE BBC'S SPARE PARTS

We undertook another project around this time for Talbot Motors of Coventry, formerly Chrysler UK. Talbot's spare parts business needed a new name as the old name had been retained by Chrysler, the former owners of Talbot. We were given the job of developing this new name, though we were told that all legal searches would be handled internally – we would have no responsibility whatever for these. Accordingly, we conducted the name creation and testing phases and a bunch of names were shortlisted by the company's marketing team and passed to their existing advisers for searching.

We were told a few weeks later that the name for their car parts business, which they had chosen from our list of recommendations, was to be Carfax. In fact, I liked it very much. It was appropriate, distinctive and the incisive final 'x' gave it graphic strength. However, a few days later, I read an article in a Sunday paper announcing that the BBC was to launch an in-car warning system under the name Carfax. It was a system, then novel, which interrupted the radio signal and informed motorists of problems in the area. I discussed this development with Mike Grant and he said that if the BBC had got there first it could be a real problem for Talbot as they were marketing car radios. He said he hoped they were aware of the BBC's plans and had reached an arrangement with the BBC. I sent the newspaper cutting to my client, the marketing director of Talbot, and thought no more about it. I felt I was probably being alarmist, but, in any case, it was not my problem as we had not conducted the legal searches.

Many weeks later my client phoned me. He said there had been a major disaster. The company's advisers had indeed come across the BBC's registration of Carfax when they had conducted their searches but had decided it was not relevant. Later, the BBC noticed that Talbot's trade mark applications included car radios etc. and had politely written to Talbot pointing out their existing registrations and saying that there was a measure of conflict between their earlier applications and Talbot's new applications. Talbot's response had been aggressive and unhelpful. This had annoyed the BBC's legal department and a day or two before the launch of the new Carfax spares operation, the BBC told Talbot they were applying for an injunction. Talbot had no choice but to find another name as fighting the injunction would take many months and there was, in any case, no certainty they would win, in fact the reverse. The cost of the write-off of stock bearing the name Carfax, all now unusable, was huge, or so I was told.

We therefore undertook a new creation exercise without charge, though we were not at all at fault. But, as before, we were not to conduct the searches. Our friend, the marketing director, later phoned to say that one of our new names had been cleared – Motaquip – but in view of the debacle last time round, could we discreetly double check all the search results if he sent them to us? We agreed to do so and Mike Grant concluded that the name was clear insofar as the trade mark registers were concerned but we hadn't been sent any company name searches. Where were they? These needed to be checked too. I phoned to ask for them and was told that no such searches had been undertaken. We said that these really were necessary. We were asked to carry them out, but simply as a precaution.

But, we discovered two serious problems – a medium sized chain of car parts retailers in the West Midlands and a smaller chain in the North of England, each with a very similar name. If Talbot had gone ahead with the launch of Motaquip without sorting out these problems, they might well have been in deep trouble. We reported this back and were asked to conduct confidential investigations and, if possible, negotiate to sort out any problems. We were given a virtually unlimited budget to buy off both of these third parties. In the event, after a great deal of sleuthing, we were able to purchase the rights from one of the companies for £1,000 and from the other for a little more plus the cost of reprinting a few pieces of literature. Talbot was unbelievably lucky and the credit for sorting out a potentially very serious mess went in large part to Novamark and in particular to Mike Grant.

MADISON AVENUE

Every assignment was, as I have mentioned, different and our clients tended to be generous and supportive. Mars, for example, a company with a formidable reputation, gave us lots of work in both the naming and the legal areas. Indeed, it was Mars who strongly encouraged me to open an office in the US as they said they had lots of work for us there.

By 1979, the year we opened in New York, the Metro had been launched and our UK business was picking up. But I was worried that all the publicity we were generating in the UK would lead some entrepreneurial American to start a similar business in the potentially huge US market and I would miss out on the real prize.

In May 1979 I decided to accompany Mike Grant to the annual US trade mark convention in Palm Beach, Florida. I already knew the US quite well, but wanted to learn more about the American trade mark scene. I flew with Laker Airways to Miami, but my flight was late and I missed my connection up the coast to Palm Beach. With three others, also going to the convention, I took a taxi north. As we drove up the interstate highway we passed Fort Lauderdale, Boca Raton and other coastal cities. Each had a huge domestic airport next to the highway and all of them were littered with private jets. The US was a honeypot, it was clear, and we needed to do business there. This impression was reinforced at the conference. After dreary, rundown Britain it was stimulating to meet the executives responsible for the worldwide trade mark affairs of Coca-Cola, Procter & Gamble, Kimberly-Clark and Visa. I told them what we were doing in London and they all seemed to think that if we opened in the US, their companies could make use of our services.

On the last day of the conference I phoned my sister, Eileen, in London, and she told me that things there were fairly quiet. So, I purchased a ticket to New York arriving on a Saturday night. On the Sunday morning I bought a copy of the *New York Times* and went through the classified ads looking for offices and office equipment suppliers. On the Monday morning I called one of the advertisers and took a cab to a small office suite at East 61st Street and Madison, near to where Barneys is now located.

The offices were on the top floor of a brownstone and they had a spare room. A former Hollywood actress, turned headhunter, occupied the remainder of the offices. I agreed to rent this spare office and we would also pay to share the reception area, boardroom and the cost of the receptionist. That afternoon I visited a firm of lawyers and instructed them to incorporate a new business. The following day I went round office equipment suppliers on the Lower East Side and bought office furniture, a filing cabinet and a swish IBM golfball typewriter. On the Wednesday, I queued up at the Laker offices nearby and bought a ticket home. We now had a US business – I had deliberately dropped myself in it. If I hadn't taken the plunge and signed a lease, I might have messed around for years. Now I was committed. I needed to be, but was it a step too far?

WHO'S THE DADDY?

I must now reveal a matter of some embarrassment, being in the naming business. You will recall that I started Novamark in the UK, in partnership with a French company of the same name. For the couple of years or so after I started my business in London, I received increasingly urgent calls from Novamark Paris asking for money. For example, if we were undertaking a Europe-wide creation exercise, and they had helped out with the name creation and the language checking, they would ask if they could possibly invoice me for a disproportionately large part of the fee. They would, they said, pay me back in due course but they urgently needed to issue an invoice and get some cash in. I was worried – we were not at all flush with cash ourselves – but helped as much as I could. Then one day their phones weren't answered and eventually I reached Jean-Yves Fornis, the managing director, at his home to ask why. He said that Novamark Paris had gone bust. He apologised profusely for all the money he had 'borrowed' and not paid back, but I knew he had been acting in good faith so I couldn't feel too bad. He gave me the name of the liquidators and that was that.

I wrote to the liquidators saying that I was owed money by Novamark Paris and pointed out too that Novamark Paris owned part of Novamark London, and I was prepared to buy this back. I also said I would buy the Novamark name worldwide. I received no reply. Our solicitors also wrote, again nothing was heard. We then exercised our rights under the company's articles to buy back the minority shareholding in light of the liquidation of the French company. However, our cheque to the liquidators was never cashed and we never had a reply to any of our further letters. After a couple of years I largely forgot about my former partners.

Then I had a mysterious phone call from Paris. It came from a man called Pierre-Louis Chereau, owner of Cabinet Chereau, a large French trade mark practice. He said I must come to see him on a matter of great urgency and insisted that we meet first thing the next morning in Paris. He wouldn't tell me what it was about. Reluctantly, I took the earliest flight to Paris from Heathrow and got to his office before 10am local time. His secretary sat me down on a narrow chair outside his office door and said he would be with me in a few minutes. By 10.30am he had still not appeared. I was furious and said I would leave but the secretary begged me to stay. Eventually just before 11am, Chereau came out. I asked him why he had been so ill-mannered as to insist I got up at four o'clock in the morning British time to take a flight to Paris and then kept me waiting for an hour outside his office. First he said that he had had someone in his office with him but I pointed out there was only one door and I had been sitting outside it and no one else had emerged. He then said that I 'must not get upset with my new daddy'. I asked him what he was talking about, saying that my father had died some years earlier so I had no 'daddy'. He then told me that he had bought the assets of Novamark Paris from the liquidators and as Novamark London was a subsidiary, he now owned my business.

We had a magnificent ding-dong. I pointed out that Novamark Paris did not own a single share in my business and had only ever held minority and, in view of his behaviour, I did not want any kind of tie-up with his firm. Eventually, his office manager was brought in to take me to lunch (I did get something out of the trip) and I started to realise I must sever all ties with Novamark Paris. I also realised that legal proceedings in the French courts could be expensive and protracted. I was presented with a serious naming problem of my own.

I did not tackle the problem immediately. I had no plans at that stage to operate in France and I owned the Novamark name in the countries of interest to me. However, once I decided to open an office in the US, I knew I had to grasp the nettle. I continued to use the name Novamark in the UK for a little longer, but in the US we quickly adopted the new name Interbrand. Over the course of the next couple of years we developed Interbrand as our worldwide brand. We were no longer called Novamark.

We developed the name Interbrand in-house, of course, and tested it and cleared it on an international basis. Equally importantly, we were beginning to view ourselves as a broadly based consultancy, not simply a naming company, and a branding consultancy at that. The word 'brand' was very little used at the time, but we knew even then that our business was now all about brands, not just about names or trade marks, and realised that we should overtly acknowledge this.

WORKING WITH 'THE PROFESSIONALS'

Another area of embarrassment involves our then fully owned trade mark law subsidiary, Grant & Co, run by my colleague, Mike Grant. Grant & Co got its business in four different ways. First, it conducted the national and international searches required by Novamark/Interbrand; second, it handled the ongoing trade mark affairs of clients who liked the way we operated and decided to switch their work to us (these included Sainsbury's, British Telecom and Ford UK); thirdly, it conducted UK work on behalf of overseas trade mark law practices especially those who were given loads of trade mark searches by us in connection with name creation projects and who felt they must give us some of their UK work to keep us sweet; and, finally, it got work, albeit not much, from the personal contacts of Mike and, later, his colleagues. When we had set up Grant & Co as an apparently separate entity, we did so knowing that several of these sources of business would be denied to us unless we presented our new trade mark practice as a 'real' practice with a legal-sounding name. Mike however held all his shares in the parent company, not in the fully owned subsidiary, and we all agreed that 'Grant & Co' was really a marketing device and not a separate business with its own separate personality and culture. 'Grant & Co' was intended simply as a different trading style, that was all.

In retrospect, however, calling the practice Grant & Co was a mistake and not one I would make again. The business became a successful and highly influential trade mark practice, one of the fastest growing in its sector, almost entirely due to the name creation business and the work and contacts which this generated. As the business grew, we recruited more trade mark professionals. The first was Adrian Spencer, so Grant & Co became Grant Spencer; then John Caisley joined and Grant Spencer Caisley emerged, and so forth. After a few years I realised that our trade mark law practice had little interest in name creation or brand development, as it had more than enough business to keep it busy from the likes of Mars, J. Sainsbury, Ford UK, British Telecom and from overseas associates.

Worse, there was an emerging culture within the practice that meant that, as 'professionals', they were increasingly embarrassed for 'their' practice to be associated with coarse marketing people like me. Mike and his colleagues eventually proposed to me that they swap their stakes in Interbrand for 60% of Grant Spencer Caisley and I eventually agreed to this, though we retained various controls. Later, we sold out completely and started a second trade mark practice, Markforce Associates to replace the Grant & Co practice. This was not the name of the principal, so professional egos were this time kept under control. We had learned our lesson.

BUFFALO IN THE WINGS

My third and final embarrassment from around this time is Buffalo Discount Warehouses. After I left Queensway, a former colleague, Duncan Reekie, whom I had recruited from Marks & Spencer to be Queensway's buying director, suggested that we start our own discount furniture and carpet chain, which he would manage. I agreed.

We quickly built up a small chain of warehouses under the name Buffalo, as well as a number of specialist carpet shops called Carpet City. Duncan and I gave personal guarantees on the new outlets, all of which were leased. These guarantees made for increasingly sleepless nights, but we did not anticipate this at first.

In the 1980s, however, Britain was hit by a severe retailing recession as the housing market collapsed. Duncan and I started to realise that Buffalo could fail and, if it did so, we would both be wiped out. The problem was how to get out unscathed. Fortunately, Phil Harris wanted to purchase certain units of ours and we knew we could find buyers for others. The offers from Harris and others were not particularly good, but they gave us the opportunity to exit reasonably smoothly. We then put the company into solvent voluntary liquidation. This process, though smooth, was much more painful than I had ever imagined and dented my confidence.

The experience of dealing with P.L Chereau in Paris, the Grant & Co problem in the UK and the liquidation of Buffalo did, however, teach me a lot!

BACK TO INTERBRAND

It took me some years to see my name creation consultancy as anything other than an engaging and diverting boutique business. My initial reason for getting into this business was to escape from Dunlop and from big business and it was the best idea I could come up with. Later, I began to think that I might be able to open a series of small international subsidiaries, all doing naming and co-operating on creative work and language checks. The limit of my vision by the late 70s/early 80s was an international chain of six or eight name creation businesses each employing no more than ten or a dozen people. But the failure of Buffalo re-energised me and I came to realise that Interbrand was my best chance of business success. By 1982 I began to entertain some even grander notions of what Interbrand might become.

6

MR X AND WENDY WEE

In which I took the plunge and started an international network called Interbrand.

I formed our subsidiary in New York in 1979 and my first priority, once I refocused on Interbrand, was to get this firmly established. For the first year or so I managed the New York office from London as best I could. I became one of Laker's best trans-Atlantic customers, flying back and forth every couple of weeks. We carried out much of the groundwork for our New York business in London. For example, I prepared New York business brochures in London and flew them over in my baggage.

I also bought directories and other lists from which Eileen in London, and my part-time assistant/receptionist in New York, typed up address labels. We blitzed American businesses with our mailshots and I also secured great PR in the US marketing and business press. *The Wall Street Journal*, for example, ran a terrific story on us. Whenever we got an enquiry I would try to deal with it as if I was sitting in New York, even though, in many instances, I was thousands of miles away. I didn't pretend I was where I wasn't, I just didn't happen to mention that I was speaking from London.

It was all rather haphazard and amateurish, but fortunately it worked. The good thing about name creation is that there is always somebody out there who is in a fix, who has just found that his beloved, chosen name is registered by somebody else or who is about to launch a new product and can't find a name he likes. I won a couple of projects in our first year and this was just enough to keep us going and pay the major bills.

At the same time I was looking for someone to run the US business. I considered recruiting somebody in the UK and moving them to New York, but realised that this would be a horrendously expensive and uncertain proposition. But then, I was introduced to a man called David Wood. David was a Brit who had moved to New York many years previously with the hotels division of Grand Metropolitan, but tired of the hotel business and was ready for a change. I liked that he knew the American scene well; Americans found him comfortable to deal with and we got on well together too. David joined me in 1980 and I gave him a large chunk of the equity of the new American business. Over the next few years the US subsidiary took off.

I loved going to New York and working on an international stage. I also liked having new overseas colleagues. I had found working on my own or in a very small office quite lonely. I liked the camaraderie of a somewhat bigger organisation. Moreover, once the US office was up and running, it became increasingly apparent that if we were to be credible as the creators of international brand names, we needed to be a truly international business, so in 1982 I opened offices in Paris and Frankfurt and in 1983 in Tokyo; offices in Milan, Seoul, Johannesburg, Sydney, Chicago and San Francisco followed.

MR X

Opening the Paris office was, in part, an act of defiance in the face of Pierre-Louis Chereau's behaviour a few years earlier, but for some time he had the last laugh, though he didn't know it. I advertised in the French marketing press for a president for my soon-to-be-formed company and had many applicants. I took a small suite at the Ritz Hotel in the Place Vendôme and over the course of a couple of days interviewed a shortlist of ten prospects.

Eventually I made an appointment, let's call him Mr X. He was an older and very elegant French executive who seemed to have all the right experience. I checked his references and it was only in retrospect that I realised there was a distinct reserve among respondents. We took lovely offices in Neuilly, an elegant suburb of Paris and they were always filled with vases of flowers and the smell of fresh coffee. He bought himself a nice motor car at company expense as, he assured me, how one presents oneself is critical to doing business in France. He spent time in London and in New York to learn the ropes and soon we were enjoying a flurry of PR and were sending many potential customers our leaflets and mailshots.

Unfortunately, it took me over a year to realise that Mr X did not have an altogether firm grip on reality. We heard of major accounts he had won but which then never materialised; they were talked about for months until the talk fizzled out. We heard of his extraordinary car smash in which many people had died but from which he had been fortunate to walk away intact (he was, however, off work for weeks, of course). He told us of a huge contract he was just about to win from the Texas subsidiary of a French business, which necessitated his flying to Texas first class to pick up the assignment (of course, it never happened). I even believed him for a while when he told me that he was being consulted by French government ministers on issues of branding and identity. Even now, I'm sure he believed every word, but it was almost all fiction and we lost a fortune. After a year I mothballed the business, though we started it up again some years later and it then did well.

CARTOGRAPHY IN GERMANY

My attempt to start a business in Germany was a little more successful but not much. As an ex-geographer, I studied the map and decided that the place to be was Frankfurt. As with Paris, I advertised widely for a managing director offering a generous salary, part of the equity and a stimulating, fun job.

I then hired a suite in the Intercontinental and conducted a series of interviews. The general standard of the candidates was utterly woeful. I can remember that few wore business suits – plaid trousers, short-sleeved polycotton shirts and seersucker jackets seemed to be the order of the day. Several of the candidates wore curious grey shoes with Velcro fastenings; a type of footwear I had hitherto only seen in care homes for the elderly.

My candidates seemed to comprise the detritus of the German economic miracle. Even thirty years later I don't understand why. Do Germans not respond to job ads? Or were they so loyal to the big companies that they didn't want to work for small companies, or for foreigners? Or were Germans of that generation simply not entrepreneurial? In any event, the field was very thin. However, we had one promising applicant, a woman who was a former senior manager at one of Germany's largest marketing services businesses. After a couple of interviews and a careful check of her references, she was appointed.

My hopes ran high, but not for long. She was exceptionally meticulous in the choice of offices, office equipment and her personal motor car – as in France, it seemed that no respectable manager could be seen in anything other than a top of the range machine. I recall that the special fire extinguisher, which fitted under the passenger seat of her new Mercedes Benz, appeared to be more valuable on its own than the seven-year-old car that I drove in the UK. She also developed an early propensity to argue with everyone else in the company. For example, if I was on a trip and called my secretary in London to ask her to send a note round to the London, New York, Paris, Frankfurt and, later, Tokyo offices, she would utterly ignore it. She was not prepared to receive instructions from or through a secretary or, indeed, anyone else in the company except me.

Nonetheless, we won a reasonable amount of new business in Germany and all the offices provided assistance with name creation and language checking. Unfortunately, in spite of our advice, my new managing director always felt she knew better. Her command of English was quite limited yet she insisted on recommending names to clients for international use, which we had advised her against. On several occasions we had serious problems where she had advocated a potential name only for me to say that there was no way whatsoever that it could be used internationally. Her standard response was to insist that 'her' name was brilliant and clearly, by implication, I didn't know what I was talking about! Our relationship did not last very long.

BREAKFAST WITH SELINA SCOTT

Our new subsidiary in Japan proved, however, to be altogether more successful and much more fun. For some years Interbrand based a lot of its PR on horror stories such as the Mitsubishi Starion. We had an amusing 'black museum' at our offices in London containing examples from around the world of inappropriate names – Pschitt lemonade from France and Krapp toilet paper from Sweden, for example. Though we did not go out of our way to pillory the Japanese, several of the best examples came from Japan.

Our black museum became extremely popular with journalists and always led to a good story. On several occasions I appeared on national television in the UK with exhibits from the black museum. One time, for example, I was interviewed on British breakfast TV by Selina Scott. She clearly didn't function too well that morning and, reading her autocue, introduced me as a man who had a business making seamless guttering.

When I said that no, I was the man who made up brand names, she looked utterly bewildered and signalled to me madly to keep going as she had not the slightest idea who I was.

On the table in front of me I had examples of strangely named products and launched into a story about how product naming was important and how companies often got it wrong. I picked up one or two products to illustrate the points I was making. As she slowly recovered her composure she tentatively picked up another of the exhibits and asked what it was – it was Super Piss spray de-icer for car locks, sold in Finland. She clearly didn't quite understand why the name was funny and looked totally bemused, especially when I commented that the natural product was rumoured to be better than the canned variety. The camera crew cracked up and started guffawing off screen. After four or five minutes of free publicity the interview was ended. Later that month the interview was selected for Pick of the Month and some time after that it was featured in the special Pick of the Year programme. For a small company like ours, such publicity was invaluable.

And it wasn't just in the UK that we received such publicity. As soon as we started our business in the US, I mailed some of the products from our black museum to Jay Leno in Hollywood. I had not previously heard of the Jay Leno late night show on US TV but had become an avid viewer on my many trips to New York. A day or two after receiving the products, his producer rang to say that they were structuring a programme around them and he would be sure to credit Interbrand, which he did. Jay Leno ran similar programmes on a number of occasions and for such a small company, we became wonderfully well known in the US.

LOST IN TRANSLATION

Japanese businesses are even more sensitive about how they present themselves internationally than western businesses. Maintaining face is of critical importance and Japanese newspapers were not slow to pick up stories of Japanese heavy-handedness in the naming of international products. We had had a number of enquiries through our London office from Japanese companies, but found it difficult to secure assignments without a Japanese presence. By 1983 I was convinced that we had a strong opportunity in Japan. I spent several months reading up on how to do business in Japan and concluded that we really needed a joint venture partner in that difficult market. Using reference works and with help from the British Trade Commission in Tokyo I compiled a list of potential partners from among the many market research agencies, design companies and marketing services businesses located there. I particularly favoured as potential partners Western businesses with Japanese offices as I felt that communications would be easier with them and that culturally they would be a better fit. I wrote to about fifty of these telling them about Interbrand and setting out our plans for the Japanese market. I explained that we were looking for a joint venture partner to work with. Each side would contribute 50% of the capital. We would contribute product and marketing know-how, whereas our partner would be expected to contribute contacts and experience in the Japanese market. We received quite a number of interested responses and I planned my first trip to Japan to meet potential partners.

I had always wanted to visit Japan, but knew little about the country. I can still remember my feeling of excitement on the journey there. At that time most airlines were unable to overfly Siberia, so the flight seemed never ending as it went via the Gulf, India, Hong Kong and Taiwan. It took almost twenty-four hours and I was exhausted on arrival. I don't think I had ever arrived anywhere so strange. Narita Airport was sophisticated, modern and efficient, but utterly unfamiliar.

The bus trip from the airport to the hotel was full of fascinations – the way in which the bus pulled up within an inch of its designated spot, precisely where we had been told to form a queue; the baggage assistant who wore a white mask because he had a head cold; the way in which the driver bowed to his passengers while wearing white gloves and a business suit; the huge security presence around the airport; the clipped topiary; the 'love hotels' on the edge of town; the brutish flyovers and glaring neon; the exquisite modern buildings cheek by jowl with concrete monstrosities; everything. It was like arriving on another planet rather than another country. The film *Lost in Translation*, starring Bill Murray, captures it well.

The next morning at breakfast, heavily jetlagged, I started to meet potential new partners. I was impressed with the talent available and was confirmed in my decision to seek a western business as a partner. However, most such western companies seemed to have rather shallow roots in Japan. They were staffed by people from Britain, the US or Australia who had been in Japan for only a few years at most and did not speak much Japanese.

Few of them had any Japanese clients at all; they were mainly concerned with helping western businesses get into the Japanese market and not with Japanese companies trying to get into western markets. I met some very bright and interesting people, but needed a partner much more firmly based locally.

I found this partner in a business, run by a Harvard-educated American, which for thirty years had helped the top Japanese businesses prepare English language versions of their annual reports. Senior Japanese executives considered such annual reports to be extremely important, and companies were prepared to invest hugely in them. They demanded perfect text, exquisite design and fine photography – the President of Toyota or Sony had to have an annual report as impressive as that of his opposite number at Ford or IBM. The company provided such a service and had the market sewn up. They employed a couple of hundred staff, about half of them western, including account executives, writers and designers. They were intrigued by Interbrand and had been looking for new opportunities for some time. We decided to form a joint venture company, Interbrand Japan, and they assigned two of their best people to it, Terry Oliver, a Brit who had lived in Japan for almost twenty years and spoke and wrote fluent Japanese, and Harada-san, an excellent Japanese account executive. Terry and Harada-san turned out to be fantastic new colleagues – Terry became CEO of Interbrand Japan and later of Interbrand Asia Pacific – and from the outset I realised that our new venture was going to do well.

THE BLACK MUSEUM

I should speak a little more about Interbrand's so-called black museum because, even though we were all thoroughly tongue-in-cheek about its significance, it generated huge interest. Our collection of weird and wonderful product names received exposure around the world in press articles and on TV and radio shows. Indeed, a check on Google reveals that the strangely named brands we introduced to the world all those years ago still command a great deal of interest and still provoke much amusement.

In the food and drink sector (mainly), I remember venerable (as well as scurrilous and even juvenile) examples such as Sic and Pschitt, both soft drinks from France (the latter has an interesting onomatopoeia of opening a carbonated drink container); Plopp, a Swedish caramel chocolate bar, which is, I am told delicious; Sweat, a sports drink from Japan designed to replace sweat and Kunto, a health product from Finland (the brand owner also produced Kunto Plus.)

Then there was Turd Baby, the Taiwanese equivalent of the Kinder Egg; Spankers, a syrup cake from Holland and Bum! Turkish biscuits. I could go on and on.

Of course, to be entirely fair, the owners of these products probably never intended them to be marketed internationally. But then, they could not have done, had they wanted, could they?

But the traffic is not entirely one way. There are, for example, significant differences between American English and British English. In the US, a fanny pack is a belt pack. We do not use fanny packs in Britain, as far as I know. Similarly, the tenant in the next-door suite of offices to ours in New York was a Dr Wank. Visitors from the London office found this amusing beyond belief but US colleagues were bewildered by our amusement. What had we found so funny?

Curiously, it now seems that new entrants to Interbrand's collection in its black museum get fewer every year. Could it be that the message about the need for international language checking, first put out by Interbrand all those years ago, has hit home?

TOM BLACKETT AND WENDY WEE

While I was dashing around the world, trying to establish businesses in New York, Paris, Frankfurt, Tokyo and elsewhere, I was also concerned to ensure that Interbrand thrived in the UK. After all, the funding for all these new businesses had to come from the UK business. Fortunately, the Metro naming project for Austin Rover had given us a huge boost as far as name creation was concerned and our trade mark law activities provided us with a steady, reliable source of income. Thus, throughout the early 1980s the UK business became steadily busier though all the profits we earned in the UK were eaten up elsewhere. I could not afford, therefore, to hire lots of new people in the UK so most of the name creation projects in the home market as well as the job of developing an international business fell to me. I was rushed off my feet but it was exhilarating.

Our core Interbrand service at that time remained name creation, though trade mark law was an important adjunct. As we grew, however, I increasingly fretted that we needed to become more sophisticated in what we did. Our international offices helped us offer a better service but I still felt that our capabilities needed improvement in the research and testing areas. I therefore approached a market research business whom I had heard had special skills in the testing of names and logos. I enquired if they could assist us with our projects and one of their executives, Tom Blackett, visited me to discuss a market research 'package', which we could jointly offer to clients. Tom and I got on well and we worked together on a couple of assignments. He then told me that he was fascinated by our concept and if the opportunity ever arose, he would like to be considered as part of the Interbrand team. I offered him a job at once and, for the first time, I had a competent colleague in name creation who could provide essential back up, especially when I was travelling. He also brought particular skills in the area of market research and, most importantly, he proved great fun to work with.

Tom looks like a regular, serious, utterly composed businessman. He is always immaculately turned out and presents himself well with fluency and humour. He is a great companion with whom to go on a trip and is always positive and supportive. His unique quality, however, which only emerges when you have known him for some time, is that he does not have a serious bone in his body. When Tom is looking serious and thoughtful, you learn that he is composing some screamingly funny anecdote. His powers of mimicry are also embarrassingly good. I came to realise quite quickly that Tom could mimic our clients so well, picking up on small quirks and expressions, that the next time I met them, I couldn't keep a straight face as he had captured them to a T. I had to ask him not to mimic anyone as it could lead to great embarrassment for me.

Tom can find something funny in almost any situation and as there is so much that is absurd and amusing in business in general, and marketing in particular; we found plenty to entertain us. For example, not long after Tom joined, we were conducting an international project for Singer. They had developed a completely new range of sewing machines and wanted to use a different brand name for each part of the range in order to provide personality and consumer interest – letters and numbers were a bit dull. They had conducted a vast market research exercise and had developed 'profiles' of the typical users for each sector, for example, the professional seamstress, the enthusiastic amateur, the 'don't-give-a-damn' slob and so forth. But they had gone further; each of these had been given a nickname. Tom and I sat through an earnest and interminable presentation by Singer's market research agency, culminating in the revelation of all these nicknames – Polly Pro, Betty Bee, and so on, and one type of user that they had called, ludicrously, Wendy Wee. I could hardly keep a straight face when Tom put on his ultra serious expression. Fortunately, we each managed to contain ourselves, but only until we got outside.

With Tom on board, I had found a kindred spirit and Interbrand developed a very particular internal culture – we took our work seriously, but ourselves and the absurdity of much of business life, less so. Thinking up names for products, services and companies is a delightful and engaging way of earning a living. I had always felt that and was grateful to Tom that he shared this view. Enjoying our jobs did not demean the service we offered or insult our clients. Indeed we were passionate about the quality of what we offered and were always determined to give the best possible advice, even if we thought it might be unpalatable. But taking what we did seriously did not mean that we couldn't have fun along the way.

7

THE BIRTH OF BRANDING

In which I realised that no one had developed a service to help in the creation of brands and we named biscuits called Hobnobs.

In 1983, shortly after Tom joined Interbrand, we decided to organise a major marketing conference in London. I was increasingly miffed that we had never been invited to speak at the innumerable conferences held by the advertising and marketing community. We received a great deal of media exposure, but I suspected that, insofar as the marketing industry was concerned, we remained some sort of freak show. (I now realise that we were ignored because it was easier to prepare programmes using the same old topic and the same old speakers. We were not ignored for any other reason than that conference organisers are often idle and not very well informed. Paradoxically, within a few short years I and my colleagues were speaking at around a hundred conferences a year and we all came to loathe them.) Anyway, I was determined that we should elbow our way into the marketing mainstream.

We decided, accordingly, that we would organise a conference of our own on name creation and trade mark law: we would not wait to be invited. Consequently, we started to search for a partner. We chose the Institute of Marketing. Their conferences manager was a delightful man called Harold Shilling. He was enthusiastic about the topic but insisted that, for commercial reasons, we should hold a two-day conference and not the one-day event we had originally planned. We feared that we didn't really have enough material to cover one day, let alone two, but we did not let this deter us. We knuckled down and put together a cracking good two-day programme and I agreed to chair it.

So, what did we put into the programme besides name creation and trade mark law? We decided to include the counterfeiting of trade marked goods (Vince Carratu, an ex-Scotland Yard detective and expert in the field, agreed to speak), new product development (Tom Blackett of Interbrand and Graham Benton of the Initiatives Group were the speakers), packaging design (Mervyn Kurlansky of Pentagram), corporate identity design (John Diefenbach of Landor), the role of trade marked products in the pharmaceutical industry (Barbara Sudovar, formerly of Pfizer), retail branding (Terry Leahy of Tesco, soon to become Tesco's managing director) and a dozen or so other interesting topics with equally distinguished speakers. We were delighted with the stimulating programme we had put together and pleased with the turnout from the industry – we had well over one hundred delegates.

I remember listening with rapt attention to the various speakers because most of the subjects were as new to me as to the delegates. It slowly dawned on me, during the course of the two days, that our, that is Interbrand's, world should not simply be that of name creation, trade mark law and some limited name testing. In fact, it plausibly should embrace packaging design, corporate identity, brand strategy advice, brand licensing, market research and many of the related disciplines. Our view of our role had been far too narrow. We had a much wider opportunity than any of us had ever recognised. I believed we would be mad not to seize it.

DESIGNING THE FUTURE

After the conference we held an internal meeting at a beautiful converted mill, deep in the forest, two hours' drive north of Toronto, Canada, to discuss our embryonic group's future strategy. I put to my colleagues my new, expanded vision for Interbrand – that we should turn ourselves into a broadly based consultancy. Those from London and Tokyo were uniformly enthusiastic but the response from New York and Frankfurt was much more muted; Paris did not seem to have a view. I did not want to take the group off in a new direction without the support of all my colleagues. However, in spite of certain voiced reservations, I felt I received a sufficient mandate to allow me to explore new opportunities. Even if a couple of my colleagues had been a little negative at the outset, they would come round, or so I reckoned.

Packaging and corporate identity design were immediate areas of interest. When companies spend their marketing pounds or dollars, probably

80% or more of their budget goes on advertising. The next biggest area of expenditure is usually market research, followed by design, and then by the odds and sods, including name creation. By targeting design we might not be getting into the really big money, but we were certainly heading up the food chain.

I had another reason for taking on the world of design. By 1983, Interbrand London was handling thirty to forty important name creation assignments each year, all of which had, potentially, a design component. On a number of occasions, clients we had worked with to develop a new name had asked, on completion of the naming assignment, if we would handle the packaging or the corporate identity design. They were comfortable working with us, liked our approach and knew we were, by this stage, conversant with their project, having been thoroughly briefed, met their people, toured their factories, studied their market research and organised consumer focus groups. They preferred to continue working with us rather than start all over again with a new design company. For some years I had resisted getting involved in design as I wanted design practices to refer their naming assignments to us, though this never seemed to happen. So I developed a list of preferred design suppliers with a summary of their expertise, clients and references and full contact details. Whenever a client asked us to undertake design work for them, I declined, but gave them a list of companies they might consider. We did not expect or ever receive commissions or introductory fees for doing so.

I could not, however, help noticing that the design companies we introduced to clients, and often briefed on behalf of clients, normally received vastly higher fees for their work than we had done for the strategy, naming and legal work. If we charged, say, £20,000 for a new corporate name, a design company might charge five times this amount or more for the corporate identity design. I can't say that I resented this – it was the way of the world – but I felt at times that the design stage was an 'implementational' activity which did not deserve to be so lavishly rewarded.

What really got up my nose, however, having introduced masses of good design work to design practices across London, was to discover one day, when reading *Campaign*, the advertising industry trade magazine, that two of these design companies had coincidentally, both in the same week, announced they were setting up their own naming agencies in competition with us! Both design companies claimed that they could offer a one-stop shop, unlike existing naming agencies, in other words, Interbrand. Why bother with a naming consultant? They could do the lot. I was outraged, particularly as neither had had the decency to tell me of their plans. Taking on the design industry had for me, as a consequence, a certain piquancy.

We decided, accordingly, to set up our own design practice in London. I hired a creative director, and some talented designers, and started to offer design services to our clients, but over the next couple of years progress was fairly slow. Eventually, we decided that we needed to make an acquisition and use the skills and experience of the acquired company to establish ourselves internationally. We looked, without success, in the UK – this was a time when the design industry took itself pretty seriously and there were no bargains to be had, in fact the reverse – and instead decided to make an acquisition in the US. The acquisition was far from successful but more of this later. Suffice it to say that over the course of two or three years, we learned quite a bit about the design business and grew increasingly confident that it was an activity that truly fitted our skill set. Soon we had small design studios not just in London but in New York, Frankfurt and Tokyo too. Over the coming years our design practice grew hugely and by the mid 1990s our combined design activities employed over two hundred people. We were truly in the design business and doing great work.

Name creation, trade mark legal services and design (which included corporate identity, packaging and, in time, retail design) were not, however, the only services we offered. Increasingly we were undertaking new brand development projects (that is, the conceptualisation of a new product or service as well as the associated market research, naming, brand protection and product design), appearing as expert witnesses in court cases, sorting out portfolios of brands and advising on brand disposals. We also developed special skills in the naming and branding of pharmaceutical products.

Our 1983 London conference, in conjunction with the Institute of Marketing, was the catalyst for redefining the scope of services we would offer. From that time on, I actively sought to broaden the basis of what we offered far beyond name creation and trade mark law. But even though we soon had a broader view of our future, we were still somewhat fuzzy as to the scope of our enlarged activities. I knew that we needed to give a definition and a name – that is 'form' to the package of services we now offered, but what should that be?

PROTECTING HOBNOBS

Over the years I had come to realise, though imperfectly, that 'naming' is not simply about thinking up a snappy and 'registrable' name for a new product, service or company. The choice of name frequently creates the entire personality of the product, service or organisation and this carries through into packaging, presentation, advertising and positioning. Our role was, accordingly, far more important than mere word-smithing.

Take Hobnobs, for example, a name we developed for United Biscuits. Our original brief was to give this wonderful new biscuit a fairly banal, descriptive name that would be subordinate to the McVitie's house brand. But there was a problem: sub-brands for such products, which were overly descriptive, simply played into the hands of the supermarkets, as they were too easily copied by them for their private label products. Thus if McVitie's brought out McVitie's Chocolate Digestives, ASDA would launch ASDA Chocolate Digestives. If, on the other hand, McVitie's brought out McVitie's Chocolattas, Chocolattas might just be distinctive enough to deter ASDA from calling their product by the same name. Our brief, in the case of what became Hobnobs, was to come up with a semi-descriptive name for a new product that was just about protectable and incapable of being slavishly copied.

When conducting our consumer groups for the new McVitie's product, however, we were amazed at the response to the new biscuit. People absolutely loved it and we realised that United Biscuits potentially had a huge success on its hands. We realised, too, that to give this fantastic new product a relatively unexciting, semi-descriptive name would be to hide its light under a bushel. We put it to United Biscuits that the new product warranted and needed a much more differentiated, intrusive, freestanding and protectable name, than a semi-descriptive name like the Super-Crunch or Tasti-Bic, the sort of name they were seeking. We said that there was no reason at all why such a name could not still be presented as part of the McVitie's range; it did not conflict with the established range name. United Biscuits eventually accepted this advice and we developed the name Hobnobs for them; a name that alludes to the texture and nature of the product, but which is also cheeky and nicely alliterative. The effect of the naming exercise was to determine the entire personality of this massively successful brand. Clearly, naming in this case went far beyond mere name invention.

A NEW WORD — BRANDING

Following the London conference, and while we were busily expanding our range of services, I decided that we should try to 'capture' this new activity we were now involved with – creating, managing and protecting the 'personality' of products, services and businesses – by editing a book on the subject. Several of the speakers at our earlier conference agreed to contribute chapters for this book; others were to be written by colleagues and by outside experts. These included Leslie Collins, a psychologist specialising in market and consumer behaviour, Robert Grayson, a Professor of Marketing from New York, Dr Klaus Morwind from Henkel of Dusseldorf, and others. I thought that editing this book would be a piece of cake – I believed I would merely have to assemble a bunch of manuscripts, put a large staple through the top left hand corner, and add my name as editor. In fact, it took several years, as producing the book turned out to be a major undertaking.

About a third of the chapters I required arrived on time and were more or less suitable for publication without too much editing. A further third never arrived at all and, in desperation, I ended up writing the chapters virtually in their entirety, sending them to the 'authors' for their approval. The rest either arrived many months late or needed a huge amount of editing.

One contributor particularly annoyed me. He failed to write the chapter he had promised but I was keen to have his name as one of the authors, so I wrote it in its entirety and sent it to him. He approved the chapter but a little later when, at the publisher's request, I wrote to all the chapter authors requesting that they give me their copyright so that there was only one copyright holder, the 'author' refused to give me 'his' copyright! Later I wrote to everyone proposing that the modest royalties on the book should be given to the Oxfam charity. He agreed to this, but a couple of years later, he sent me an aggressive letter accusing me, in effect, of stealing 'his' royalties. Being an editor is not as easy as it may seem.

Fortunately, I found a publisher for the unusual book who proved to be very supportive. This publisher believed our book broke entirely new ground and recommended that I thought of a title for it that suggested what we were writing about was new and important. After some thought, I called the book *Branding: A Key Marketing Tool*. The word 'branding' had not been used before, except in cowboy movies. Consequently, it took a while to become established (more of this later) as a term denoting a business or marketing activity. But in giving the name 'branding', which we had newly coined, to the services we offered, we mapped out clearly the scope of our services – the development, measurement, management and protection of brands. In later years many people would claim to have 'invented' branding, but I have no doubt that the distinction of first giving a name, structure and shape to the concept falls to Interbrand. But, as I shall describe later, it was the 'science' of brand valuation which really lit branding's blue touch-paper.

8

LAYING DOWN THE LAW

In which I created a subsidiary business in trade mark law, lobbied parliament to introduce new legislation, became a publisher and completed our re-focusing on 'branding'.

Another area in which I was keen to expand was trade mark law and related services. The protection of intellectual property is vital to businesses; in particular, those whose principal value is intangible (for example, brand-rich businesses like Coca-Cola, P&G and Nestlé), and I knew that this would be an area of growing importance to our clients. After we divested ourselves of Grant Spencer Caisley, we started a second practice in the UK, Markforce Associates, and in due course hired a recently qualified trade mark attorney to run it called Janet Fogg. She proved to be an outstanding business manager and the practice became very successful and extremely profitable. She later joined the main board of Interbrand.

For some years we attempted to turn Markforce into an international trade mark practice, not just a UK practice. Our plan was to open a Markforce business in each of our offices so as to have a truly international capability in this area. However, the restrictive practices of the world's lawyers defeated us. In the US and Germany we discovered that it was not possible for corporations to practice law and trade mark advice was classified as a mainstream legal activity. We protested against this situation for years and probed to see whether there were any loopholes, but to no avail. Our only trade mark law practice remained in the UK.

I could understand the Germans implementing restrictive practices, as it seemed to me they have always been highly protective and attracted to cartels. However, the strength of the legal cartel in the United States, the Land of the Free, amazed me, particularly as every law practice in the US seemed to be turning itself into a Limited Liability Partnership (LLP).

They were not prepared to offer unlimited protection to their clients but they would sure as hell come down on us, a limited company, if we had the temerity to set up Markforce Associates in the US and offer 'legal services' to US companies.

A BRAND LOBBY

We decided we had to make the best of it and develop our legal activities as far as we possibly could, but not, of course, where it was illegal to do so. Our focus, in so far as trade mark law services were concerned, was accordingly, exclusively on the UK where we were determined to make Markforce a major player. Our first break came with the passing of new legislation to allow the registration and protection of trade marks for services. In the early 1980s the European Community, now the EU, held early consultations as to where the proposed Community Trade Mark Office (CTMO) might be located. As a relatively late entrant to the EU, Britain had missed out on all the major EU institutions – these were located in such cities as Brussels, Luxembourg, The Hague and Strasbourg. The Germans had bid for the European Patent Office and had just won it for Munich.

By the time Britain joined the EU only a few minor institutions were still awaiting new homes and these included the CTMO. I was surprised that the British trade mark community appeared to be doing nothing to lobby for this office, as it would have a major impact on trade mark activity in Britain. Conversely, if we were to lose it, British trade mark attorneys could be seriously disadvantaged. I spoke to one or two like-minded people in the profession and we decided to do something about it. My friend and former colleague at Dunlop, Iain Mills, had quite recently been elected Conservative MP for Meriden in the West Midlands and was Personal Private Secretary to Norman Tebbitt, one of the most senior Cabinet ministers at the time. I approached Iain and asked him if he would help us lobby for the CTMO, and he agreed to do this. He also agreed to join the board of Interbrand as a non-executive director so as to become more familiar with brands and trade marks and their increasingly important role in business.

One serious problem our lobbying efforts faced was that the British trade mark system at that time did not allow for the registration of trade marks for services, only for goods. Given that service industries were growing rapidly in importance, particularly in the UK, this was a serious omission. It was also one that other countries pointed out when lobbying for the CTMO for themselves, as by then nearly all the other EU countries had well established service mark provision.

One of the earliest meetings, which Iain had arranged as our adviser, was with a minister at the Department of Trade and Industry (DTI). This minister said that he was supportive of London's bid for the CTMO and he believed that the Prime Minister, Margaret Thatcher, was also supportive, but the decision was some way off and who knew what issues might come up in the meantime that would demand Government attention? He made it clear, without saying so in as many words, that the Government did not consider the CTMO to be a major prize; they would gladly have it if they could, but would not go out of their way to fight for it. We then put to him that if the Government did no more than stand mutely by, we had no chance whatsoever of getting the CTMO. If we wanted it, the one thing the Government could do immediately was to introduce service trade mark legislation. This would increase our chances of winning the CTMO and, in any case, was a very important initiative given that Britain was increasingly becoming a service-based economy. He considered the matter and seemed impressed by this argument, and eventually said he would do whatever he could. We were by no means hopeful, but, literally, couple of weeks later, in the Queen's Speech setting out the Government's legislative programme for the next session of Parliament, the last item, clearly tacked on at the last minute, was a statement that the Government would introduce service trade mark legislation in the next session of Parliament. Within months it was on the statute book. I am quite sure that it was our lobbying which produced this result.

TRADE MARK BONANZA

The effect of this legislation was, potentially, to increase the size of the UK market for trade mark legal services by perhaps one third or more. Not only would Britain's banks, insurance companies, household removers, travel agents, management accountants, lawyers, consultants, media buyers, advertising agencies, window cleaners and nursing homes be able to register their names as service trade marks, but service businesses around the world doing business in the UK would also be able to take advantage of the new UK legislation. We could see that for the profession, it could be a bonanza.

It was difficult, however, for trade mark practices to attract new clients from the services sector, mainly because they were prevented by their Institute from soliciting new business other than from existing clients. Moreover, the Institute itself had played no real part in lobbying for the new legislation and certainly took no interest in making potential users aware of the new legislation on behalf of all its members.

A few weeks before the new legislation came into force we realised that this presented us with an extraordinary opportunity. No one else in the trade mark business was doing anything whatsoever to publicise the new legislation or its benefits – so why shouldn't we take the lead? We knew we might be criticised for 'touting', the traditional ya-boo insult hurled at companies like Interbrand, but this didn't bother us. Furthermore, Interbrand was a marketing consultancy and not a traditional professional practice. And, besides, it was us who had worked with Iain Mills MP to get the new legislation on to the Statute Book.

Accordingly, we prepared huge mailing lists and bombarded Britain's service industries with information. Some of them made their own arrangements, but a large number placed their service trade mark filing work with Markforce. When the new service mark provisions came into effect, Markforce filed more applications than almost any other practice in Britain, even though we were one of Britain's smallest trade mark practices at that time.

Later, despite a measure of pique at our success, several firms thanked us for what we had done to raise the profile of trade marks among service businesses. One practice, however, referred me to the Disciplinary Committee of the Institute of Trade mark Agents; this didn't much concern me, as I was not a trade mark attorney! I said it was like being threatened with expulsion from a golf club I didn't belong to.

A JOURNAL FOR THE SOUK

We also ventured into publishing. I had regularly attended the annual convention of the United States Trademark Association (USTA) (you will note that it is 'trademark' to the Americans and 'trade mark', two words, to the Brits – I have always thought it curious that we all work in the area of trade marks but can't agree on a common spelling of the word itself!) and had made many friends in the profession. Even in the early 1980's, the convention attracted 3–4000 delegates each year from around the world, of whom perhaps ten to 15% would be representatives of the world's major trade mark owners (Rolls Royce, MasterCard, Philip Morris, Mercedes Benz, Heineken, Toyota, Shiseido etc.), the rest being US and foreign attorneys anxious for lucrative trade mark work.

Though it presented itself as a dignified professional gathering, it was in fact a souk where the purveyors of trade mark largesse walked tall and those seeking their business paid homage. Year after year I participated in and observed this huge, wealthy international get-together – the immaculately turned out South American attorneys, the bewildered Japanese, the Escada-clad German women lawyers and the Indian attorneys in their hopsack weave suits. It struck me that it was quite astonishing that this huge, extended, affluent group, all of whom shared a common interest, did not have a common professional journal. There were abstracts of legal cases and national newsletters, but no international journal for everyone.

One year, after my return from the convention, I decided to do something about it. I spoke to several British publishers about setting up a joint venture publishing business targeting the worldwide trade mark and intellectual property professions. None of the publishers, however, showed much interest. It then became clear that even if one of them eventually took the bait, we would be too late for the convention the next year which would be in San Diego, my preferred launch venue. I decided that we should go it alone. I came up with the name 'Trademark World' for the new publication and had our designers prepare a mock up. It had an attractive full-colour front cover, trade mark news from around the world, excellent cartoons (one of the regular participants in our name creation sessions was a well known young cartoonist who was delighted to help out in return for a two-year contract), articles on important topics from around the world (for example, the latest news on the proposed European trade mark system), case reports, display advertising and classifieds. I approached friends and appointed a distinguished panel of about twenty-five leading attorneys from around the world and was assured of a steady flow of news and information.

I was reluctant, however, to hire anyone to edit the new journal until it was established. I therefore undertook to edit the first few editions myself, as I was keen to set the tone and style of the new journal. For a few months, in addition to running Interbrand, servicing clients and travelling the world to sort out the problems in our various offices, I became a journalist. I also had to market the new journal. Again, I relied upon mailshots. The world of trade marks is awash with lists and directories, and I collected these from all over the world – attendees at conventions, members of legal organisations, journalists showing a particular interest in intellectual property matters and so on. Eventually I prepared a mailing list of several thousand potential subscribers and mailed out to each a brochure and a subscription form. A few hundred individuals and firms signed up, and we were in business.

A couple of months later I flew to San Diego, having air-freighted about 4,000 copies of the new journal ahead of me. We were not allowed to take a stand at the convention (stands were not allowed as it was considered vulgar to introduce 'commercialism' into the convention; a curious view given that trade marks are about trade, and most of the delegates attending were doing so in the hope of winning new business), so instead I went round all the convention hotels in the middle of the night and shoved a free copy of the journal under every door. The response was mixed. We got more subscriptions but there was also much sniffiness, noticeably from those who felt slighted because they were not on our editorial board. However, everyone seemed to like the first edition of *Trademark World*.

Over the next few months I prepared, published and distributed the monthly editions of *Trademark World* and it got better all the time. I found myself enjoying being a journalist and I also found the subject matter fascinating. My colleagues complained, however, that it was taking up too much of my time – my job was to run Interbrand – so I hired a distinguished former academic as the full-time editor. He was also given the brief of introducing two sister publications, *Patent World* and *Copyright World* as these two areas of the law were also without their own journals. Within a short time, we owned and published three intellectual property journals and had a major new arm to our business, as each journal had a good subscription base and lots of advertising. Then, my colleagues complained even more strongly that I was taking too much time looking after my three new babies to the detriment of more lucrative client work. I knew they were right, but it was with great regret that we sold the business a couple of years later. At least I had the quiet satisfaction of knowing that we had had a major influence on the world of intellectual property, even if most people were blissfully unaware of what we had done.

Our commitment to trade mark law as a business was a unique and differentiating part of our offering. We expected all our consultants to understand its principles and to be conversant with its practice. This gave our advice gravitas and helped to position us as a 'serious' consultancy that could legitimately command higher fees than a typical design company or 'creative' shop. And, of course, our trade mark practice continued to give us significant revenues and very attractive profits.

9

HURRICANES IN NEW YORK

In which I learnt that culture is critical to building a great business, swore that spouses could never again come along to our group conferences and learnt that I could be let down by the people I trusted.

While all this was going on, we had the problem of what Americans call 'managing the talent'.

The British business went from strength to strength from the early 1980s onwards and the Japanese business, under Terry Oliver and Haradasan, never put a foot wrong. The French business, as I have mentioned, did not get off the ground for several years. But our American and German businesses became serious headaches.

The US business started well and thrived for several years. The Anglo-American President I had recruited, David Wood, turned out to have a good feel for name creation and though he was far from being the most energetic manager in the world he was, I considered, a safe pair of hands. Our German managing director seemed also to be doing a reasonable job, though she was very difficult.

A DIFFICULT MARRIAGE

My first concerns as to underlying tensions surfaced in 1984 when we held a group conference at the beautiful Burgenstock Hotel in Switzerland. In a moment of expansiveness, never to be repeated, I had unfortunately agreed that partners could also come at company expense. This was a major mistake. One US delegate, for example, tried to leave the conference a day early, as he and his wife were tacking on to the conference a holiday in Europe. I

65

absolutely refused to allow this; our meeting was only three days long and I was damned if I was going to lose a delegate for a third of it. His wife threw a hissy-fit. We also had spouses who objected to their partners staying in the bars drinking after dinner when this, I felt, was one of the main purposes of such a meeting.

Yet another delegate, a woman from our New York office, was clearly having personal problems and rowed continually with her charming husband. She also insisted on making a massive scene at every single meal; the eggs were too hard or too soft, the wine was too warm or too cold and the soup too thick or too thin. She had a voice like a band saw and an increasingly noticeable Brooklyn accent. We all came to hate her presence. Someone remarked that it was extraordinary how expert she was on food and wine, as her standard diet in New York seemed to be corned beef sandwiches and Coke.

The most disturbing development, however, was that the principals of our New York and Frankfurt offices seemed not to participate fully in the conference. They also spent a lot of time in each other's company. I had never previously felt that there was any natural connection between them and wondered what was going on. Within months I would find out. Billings at both offices suddenly seemed to go into free-fall and I found that substantial remittances were required from London to keep each of the two businesses afloat. I went to New York a couple of times to try to get to the bottom of things, but never received a proper explanation and each time came home as worried as I had left. I could smell bad fish, but didn't quite know where the smell was coming from. Eventually I consulted lawyers and they agreed that I needed to go in, see the books, and take the appropriate action based upon hard evidence.

HURRICANES IN NYC

In mid-1985 I flew to New York. The city was on a major hurricane alert, but I felt I had to do what I had planned. I walked to the office from my hotel in 50 mph gales (they later reached 70 mph, but never became a full hurricane) and when I got there found the president of the company totally relaxed behind his desk. He said he knew he hadn't left me any choice but to confront him and why the hell had I taken so long to do it? He told me that he had given a few dollars to the reception clerk at the Ritz-Carlton on Central Park South, the hotel I always used, and he had been waiting for weeks for me to come to fire him. He was relieved when he heard I was in town. He said he'd go quietly, but, of course, we'd hear from his lawyers. At that he left, saying he would come back the next day, after the hurricane had blown itself out, to collect his personal items.

I then walked round the office to talk to everyone. One face I did not know was a young man called Chuck Brymer, then twenty-seven years old, who had joined the company only a few weeks earlier. I told all the staff that the former president had left, but said I didn't feel I had any choice but to accept his resignation as the company seemed to have gone into free-fall, though I didn't know why. The staff appeared neither upset nor surprised. I then sat at the recently departed president's desk to think over what to do for the rest of the day. Within minutes I made an interesting discovery.

Next to the desk was a large locked filing cabinet with two long drawers, which contained, I imagined, hanging files. As the filing cabinet was company property I asked the secretary to arrange for a locksmith to come round later that day to open it.

In the meantime the new recruit, Chuck Brymer, came to see me and said that he had contacted all Interbrand's active clients (there weren't very many) and told them that he was now handling their assignments, and that everything was under control. He told me that he had rearranged a couple of meetings and I could rely on him to make sure that everything went smoothly.

Later that day, after the visit of the locksmith, it was clear from the files that the former incumbent was in the process of setting up his own business in direct competition and was keen to get me to fire him. His frustration, clearly, was that I had been so slow to act. He had, however, never thought that I would look inside the filing cabinet. In the end, the material in it meant that we were able to make a clean break, with him handing back all his shares and options. I had liked him and felt desperately hurt by his behaviour, but just wanted to put it all behind me.

SPEAKING TO MY POODLE

While all this was going on, similar problems were emerging in our Frankfurt office. As I was busy on other matters I had asked Tom Blackett, my deputy chairman, to act as the main contact point for our German office, but the response from the German managing director was dismissive – she would only speak to me, not my poodle, how dare I ask Tom Blackett to speak to her, a managing director, and so on and so forth. I was so alarmed at her extraordinary, over-the-top behaviour I really thought that she was having some kind of crisis. I talked to her about my concerns and, at this, she accused me of constructive dismissal and flounced out. We were utterly bewildered as to what was going on. Tom and I flew to Frankfurt to get to the bottom of things and discovered that our former MD was also planning to set up her own company. Indeed, the former principals of our US and German offices were planning to work together to give clients the impression that each of the new businesses was really an international business. We had a major problem on our hands, or so it seemed. Luckily, neither business caused us real problems and the planned co-operation between them never materialised. Nonetheless I was much hurt by these two episodes.

A CLEAN SLATE

Fortunately over the next ten years I received nothing but loyalty from all my key colleagues and now, with the unpleasant part of my story behind me, I must introduce you to the expanding cast of key players at the company.

In 1985 we undertook an important assignment for Allied Hambro, run by Mark Weinberg, one of the most successful businessmen of his generation. Weinberg had set up an insurance business called Allied Hambro, in conjunction with Hambros Bank, and it had proven massively successful. Later, Hambro's bank sold its interest in Allied Hambro, and one of the conditions of the sale was that, after a period, Allied Hambro had to stop using the Hambro name.

What seemed like a simple job, finding a new name for the business, proved to be very difficult and emotive and we were appointed to help. We came up with the name Allied Dunbar. Our recommendation was based on the argument that the company should keep its existing logo, its existing logotype and the word 'Allied', and seek to replace Hambro with a name that was reasonably similar in length, appearance and tone. We also argued that the new name should, preferably, have some existing connection with the business. We checked the company archives and there found the name

Dunbar; it was one of the founding names of a business that had been acquired earlier. The name Allied Dunbar was accepted and launched at a huge event at the Wembley Exhibition Centre. The baton change from Allied Hambro to Allied Dunbar was virtually flawless. Policyholders, too, accepted the new name immediately and there was no upset.

Though our client on the project was Mark Weinberg, our day-to-day contact was with Michael Birkin, his young PA. Michael had studied law at London University and had later qualified as a chartered accountant with Price Waterhouse. I got on well with him and he clearly liked the way we operated. Some time later, he contacted me and asked if I was interested in his joining Interbrand; there had been changes at Allied Dunbar, he said, and his role had become less exciting. At that time, I was up to my neck sorting out problems in New York and Frankfurt and with editing *Trademark World*, *Patent World* and *Copyright World*. I also realised that managing businesses on a day-to-day basis was not my strong point. I like setting up businesses, starting new services and inventing new products, but managing businesses did not much excite me. However, experience showed close management was really needed. I proposed to Michael that he joined as Group managing director and this he did, starting in late 1986 at the grand old age of twenty-six!

Michael had an extensive network of friends, many of whom appeared to be refugees or potential refugees from the world of accounting. Several of these joined us in the coming years to help with the development of the company. All, I believe, found the atmosphere at the company stimulating and fun, and none more so than Paul Stobart, a former colleague at Price Waterhouse, who joined us about eighteen months after Michael. Paul, a Zimbabwean, had studied law at Oxford and then, after qualifying as an accountant, had worked at Hill Samuel, a merchant bank, where he specialised in corporate finance. He is, however, a marketing man to his fingertips and was fascinated by Interbrand. He proved to be an outstanding colleague, consultant and innovator, but more of that later. Both Michael and Paul, as chartered accountants, benefited from the rigour and discipline of their accountancy training and proved to be great managers and excellent consultants. Michael tightened up the management controls worldwide and drew the business together into a cohesive whole, while Paul was massively enthusiastic about branding from the day he joined and saw a future for the business which most of us hardly dared dream about.

But Interbrand was also becoming much more than a small number of principals, all on the board. We were also developing a highly competent team of account managers, many of whom are now leading lights in the world of branding. The first to join was Raymond Perrier. Raymond approached us for a holiday job when he was sixteen or seventeen – his father had been a client of ours. He came from Chelmsford, but his family originated in southern India and their original name was, I believe, Perreira, a name that reflects the Portuguese influence in that part of India. We liked him a lot; he was frighteningly bright and very lively, though at times bone-idle. He worked for us in his holidays and became an enormously popular member of the team. Later he went to Oxford to study theology, but continued subbing with us whenever he could. After graduation, he joined us full-time and quickly rose to main board level, becoming the world authority on brand valuation. After many years, he announced that he was leaving to train to become a Jesuit priest and to our astonishment, and my horror (I went to a Jesuit secondary school and loathed it – and them), he remained with the Jesuits for almost eight years and still works with them in South Africa in a lay capacity. From the intangibility of intellectual property, he moved to the intangibility of religious belief.

FINDING THE FCS

I guess that Raymond had mentioned to the appointments people at Oxford that he was joining Interbrand after graduation, and they must have logged our name with their opposite numbers at Cambridge because every year after he joined us we had a number of recent Oxford and Cambridge graduates apply and we usually took on one or two. We did not have a formal training scheme but were passionate about what we did and the quality of our work, and kept a close eye on our new recruits to make sure they made the grade. For their part, I am pretty sure that they had a great time. We treated them well, they seemed to have a lot of fun and all of them saw a great deal of the world. Raymond, for example, accumulated so many Air Miles that on his thirtieth birthday he was able to fly thirty friends to Paris for the weekend.

Another such early recruit was Andy Milligan. Andy had moved to London to attend Acting School after graduation. In order to eat, he worked for us part-time. In due course, he joined us full-time. He is perhaps best remembered for his courting of another of our small graduate team, Susannah Hart, now Mrs Andy Milligan. This transfixed the London office for months (though neither of them seemed aware of this). More recently, Andy was one of the founders of Caffeine, a strategic brand consultancy that specialises in fostering brand-led business growth and is now the clear leader in its field.

Several of our early recruits have their own branding consultancies in cities including London, New York and Amsterdam. Another, Simon Mottram, founded Rapha, the highly successful luxury brand of cycling accessories.

Collectively, our young recruits became known to us as the 'FCs', a term coined by Tom Blackett when we first considered recruiting some bright, young help. It arose because we had been working on a naming assignment and, for some reason, had been searching for names in the Dictionary of English Slang. Tom was taken with the term 'fart catcher', eighteenth century slang for a butler or servant – called this because he walked behind his master. Tom said that we really need a 'fart catcher' or two to help with the growing volume of work and 'FC' became the in-house term for these valued, talented and much-loved young recruits. Over the years 'FC' grew to become a badge of honour within Interbrand and our former FCs are now, as I have mentioned, some of the brightest and best in the marketing industry and beyond. But until recently, no one ever divulged the origin of the term FC.

When choosing FCs and other new members of staff we looked for people who were bright, hard-working, presented well and whom we thought would have an instinctive sensitivity to branding. We also insisted on a high standard of writing skills, in the belief that if someone was able to write clearly and succinctly, it almost certainly meant that they thought clearly and succinctly. In general we got it right. Over the course of ten years I don't think a single FC failed to make the grade. By contrast, we had a number of disappointments with people who joined us from ad agencies or from design companies, so much so that, after a time, we decided only to employ people from these industries in the most exceptional circumstances.

One further test that we applied to all new recruits was whether or not we would be happy to go on a business trip with them. I had had colleagues who were perfectly agreeable, but the idea of being away with them in some remote location, seeing them for breakfast, lunch and dinner each day, was horrendous. We tried to recruit people with whom it would be fun to go on a business trip and this policy led to a palpable sense of camaraderie within the company.

That sense of camaraderie and culture was critically important to us, particularly when we faced tough times, as I shall describe in a later chapter. In fact, one thing I have learned from my time in business is that 'culture' is one of the most important factors in making a business successful. Cultural fit is also, I learnt, one of the most important criteria you should apply when seeking to make an acquisition. No matter how good the deal looks on paper, if you don't 100% respect and trust the people in the company you are acquiring, you will find it a painful experience. I should have remembered this from my days observing the shambolic Dunlop-Pirelli Union in the 1970s, but I didn't. My lack of recall stung me very badly when Interbrand made its first major acquisition.

HOME RUN

As I explained earlier, we decided to grow our design activities significantly by acquiring a design practice in the US. We arranged to sell some of our shares to the venture capital business in London who held a minority stake in Interbrand in order to fund the acquisition. We had identified a suitable candidate based in Greenwich, Connecticut (in practice, almost a suburb of New York City), which also had an office in the Midwest. We knew it was probably not the best acquisition in the world, but felt it would suit us reasonably well. The firm appeared to have a strong US client base, good design skills and an impressive portfolio; we had international offices and, by that time, a really strong management team. We thought that two plus two would equal much more than five. By this time (the late 1980s) we were doing well and we paid $1 million in cash for the business with much more to follow under an earn-out arrangement should they perform. The earn-out would be paid in stock as, by this stage, we were planning to go public.

In fact, we did not choose well. A much-decorated Vietnam war veteran ran the company. He was charming and fun, but we came to realise that he was simply one of the lads and had no wish to run a business or take any personal responsibility for anything. His management colleagues were also unimpressive. Though the creative director was strong, the finance director, a former bookkeeper with an uncanny resemblance to Mr Pastry (a British comedian of the 1950s and 1960s famous for his lugubrious expression and droopy white moustache), was not. Several other members of the team seemed more interested in paid-for outings in provincial US cities than doing any real work. We started to get alarmed when the million dollar down payment slipped through the fingers of every recipient. Several bought $50,000 Rolex watches with their windfalls; another member of the team bought a 70 mph speedboat, which so scared him on its first outing, he never used it again and left it rotting in a marina.

We provided as much support as we could during the first year, but were barred from getting too involved in the business, as to do so would compromise the earn-out: we did not wish them to be able to claim that we had interfered with the running of the business, and thus made it impossible for them to make their earn-out, but they wanted the earn-out money anyway. However, we looked on with dismay at their performance even though we had the consolation that if they failed to make their earn-out we had at least bought the company at a pretty low price, though perhaps a fair one under the circumstances.

Towards the end of the first – and most important – year of the earn-out, it became clear they were not going to make any profit at all that year and would not therefore qualify for any earn-out payment – the $1 million down payment might well prove to be the full purchase price. But, we were not surprised to hear the first mutterings that 'you stopped us making our earn-out – you've got to pay us more money'. We told them that the outcome of the earn-out had been entirely in their own hands and, if we'd known a year earlier what we then knew, we wouldn't have considered them worth a fraction of what we'd already paid. It was us who should feel aggrieved, not them.

Right at the end of the year, out of the blue, they proclaimed a miracle. A large company, in California, had awarded them a huge, long-term contract – many, many millions of dollars – and had insisted that the first instalment be billed by the end of the year. This they had done, thereby saving the earn-out. They would all make a fortune, as now they had made their earn-out target and a lot more. They also tried to insist that all the revenue from the entire alleged contract should be attributed to the earn-out year. They stood to make millions.

We were happy with this development as the new contract would benefit us all, but, nonetheless, we could smell bad fish. Could this miracle really be happening? However, we insisted that only the billing made in the earn-out year would be considered for the purposes of the first year's earn-out and said this was a generous concession as none of the work had in fact been executed in that period. We had decided, under the circumstances, to be generous as we too would benefit for some years from this assignment, or so we thought.

But it was not to be. It was all imaginary. No contract had ever been awarded and even though an invoice had been prepared it had never been submitted. We spoke to the so-called client and they were mystified as to what it was all about – there had been a meeting but no assignment. We were seriously upset at this, but more was to come: we were to suffer weeks of high anxiety followed by more weeks of utter bewilderment.

So what went on? The story runs as follows. A couple of months after the episode of the non-existent contract, I received a phone call from the president of our new design company. He asked to meet me in New York on my next trip. We met a few weeks later and at this meeting he demanded that he and his colleagues receive a substantial sum of money under the earn-out, saying they wouldn't take no for an answer. I responded that they hadn't earned a penny, they had really let us, and themselves, down and I was particularly upset by the imaginary assignment at the year-end.

He leaned back in his chair, smiled and said, "John, you're not seeing this straight. You've got no choice." I asked why not. He said, "This is America. Whatever you may think, or we may think, unless you pay us the money, we'll tie you up in court for the next twenty years. You may not think you owe us any money, that's your call, but unless you pay us the money, we'll destroy your business. You can never go public with this hanging over you and nor would anyone ever buy the business, so you can do it the hard way or you can do it the easy way. Just pay up." I told him I wasn't impressed at all by his threats and behaviour. He replied, "Suit yourself." and left.

I consulted lawyers in the US and they confirmed we were in a real fix. It was an obvious 'ploy', but something must be sorted out. We were certain that no further payment was due, but the lawyers seemed to feel that we should brace ourselves to do something. But what?

Round two took place in the unlikely setting of a conference hotel in Nashville, Tennessee, home of the Grand Ol' Opry. I went there to give a paper at the annual US trademark convention. As soon as I arrived, I received a call from the president of our newly acquired design company. He had heard about my trip and wished to see me urgently to discuss matters further. The two of us met in my room at the hotel and he was perkier and friendlier than I'd ever known him. He told me that he hated the situation we were in, but business was business and he and his colleagues 'needed the money'. We talked over the issues for some time, but didn't make any progress. Eventually he told me that he was sure he could achieve a 'home run', should it come to it, so I should see sense. He then upped and left.

Astonishingly, we never heard a further word from him or anyone on his team about this matter. The subject absolutely disappeared from the radar screen and we never fully understood why. However, all trust between us had been comprehensively destroyed. Nevertheless the company's management team continued to maintain they had a fantastic business that was full of value. We responded that we differed on this, but if they were so confident as to the worth of the business, we were prepared to sell it back to them at the price we had paid them for it a couple of years earlier and which they claimed was a 'steal'. Eventually, and surprisingly, this was agreed.

We were hugely relieved to get out, but I am still mystified, even today, as to why all the confident threats suddenly evaporated. What had transpired? I have theories but no certainties. I also came to realise that acquiring 'people businesses' is a particularly risky undertaking. It really is a case of 'buyer beware'.

Interestingly, our own design practices really took off from precisely that time onwards. In the US, for example, we opened our own in-house design studio in New York within weeks of the sale of our newly acquired design practice. Within two years it was several times the size of the practice that we had bought and then lost and, in contrast, it was very profitable.

10

BRAND VALUATION

In which we fought a fierce battle to establish the financial valuation of brands, priced the true value of a loaf and transformed the way brands are viewed by the business world.

I claimed earlier that Interbrand coined the word 'branding' and, in effect, invented (or at least first recognised and described) the concept of branding. I am, however, fully aware that there may be other rival claimants to this mantle. However, surely there can be no rival claimants to my assertion that brand valuation, our second major contribution to the world of marketing, is Interbrand's alone?

In the 1980s a series of high-ticket, high-profile mergers and acquisitions took place among branded goods businesses. One such highly publicised acquisition was that by Grand Met, now Diageo, of Smirnoff. The cost of the acquisition was $1 billion, but Smirnoff only had tangible assets (i.e. freeholds, cash, stock, production facilities etc.) of $100 million. In accounting jargon, the 'goodwill' involved was therefore $900 million. At the time, the normal way of treating such goodwill was to write it off against the reserves of the acquiring company. Thus if, prior to the bid, Grand Met had had reserves of $2 billion, it would be able to add Smirnoff's tangible assets to this making $2.1 billion, but it would then have to write off the $900 million of purchased goodwill, thus reducing the company's reserves post-acquisition to $1.2 billion. In other words, the price to a company like Grand Met of buying a fabulous brand like Smirnoff was that it blew to ribbons a substantial part of its balance sheet.

Many companies disagreed with this treatment of goodwill, but until the era of the mega deals involving branded goods businesses, there was not too much incentive to alter established accountancy practice, no matter how inappropriate it was. (In fact, in the case of the Smirnoff acquisition, Grand

Met refused to write off the goodwill it had acquired, arguing that they had bought a substantial and valuable asset, the Smirnoff brand, and they were damned if they would suffer any impairment to their balance sheet, given the quality of the brand asset they had bought. The directors, therefore, attached their own valuation to the Smirnoff brand and included this value in their reserves as an intangible asset, thus minimising the damage to their balance sheet. This led to some raised eyebrows, but no one saw the makings of an accountancy revolution.)

A little later, Nestlé of Switzerland bid for Britain's Rowntree Mackintosh, huge chocolate makers of York. The night before the initial bid, Rowntree was valued on the London stock market at £1 billion and a few weeks later, after vigorous competitive bidding involving a second Swiss company and massive lobbying by the trade unions and Members of Parliament ('Don't let the Swiss take over part of Britain's heritage'), Rowntree was eventually sold to Nestlé for £2.5 billion. The City was triumphant and there was great satisfaction at the thought that the wily Swiss had been forced to pay a very full price for the company – two and a half times what they had originally bid. But there was also a realisation that companies like Smirnoff and Rowntree owned intangible assets, brands, which had been consistently undervalued or even ignored by investors and the City. These investors and analysts, always on the look-out for unrecognised value, started to take branded goods businesses much more seriously.

THE VALUE OF BRANDS

Having joined Interbrand from the Hill Samuel merchant bank, Paul Stobart was able to provide us with excellent insights into how the City viewed brands. He pointed out to us that his former banking colleagues knew virtually nothing about brands or the value of brands. Interbrand could carve out a whole new area of expertise if we were able, somehow, to give a value to brands. As chartered accountants, Paul and Michael also recognised that it was not just City bankers who knew little about brands – accountants were equally mystified. Accordingly, they were sure that we had a major business opportunity if we could somehow muscle our way into the arena.

Our chance came a few weeks after the Nestlé purchase of Rowntree

Mackintosh. I went with Paul Stobart on a trip to visit our offices in New York, Tokyo and Sydney. When we arrived in Sydney early one Friday morning, fresh off the flight from Tokyo, it was to discover that the previous day Goodman Fielder Wattie (GFW), a major Australian milling and foods group, had put in a hostile bid for Ranks Hovis McDougall (RHM), their much bigger British equivalent. Australian public interest in the bid was enormous. At the time Australia was still in the throes of its bicentennial celebrations and was starting to develop a new self-confidence. The Australian press regarded the hostile bid by GFW for RHM as the Ashes cricket series and the Rugby World Cup Final rolled into one. The prospect of giving a bloody nose to the Poms was delicious.

Paul and I saw it as Interbrand's chance. Instead of going from the airport to our hotel to shower and change, we went straight to Interbrand's offices and composed a cheeky fax to the Chairman of RHM. We said that if his company wished to retain its independence it needed to demonstrate the real value of its brands – these included Hovis, Mr Kipling, Saxa, Sharwoods and scores of others. We said that generalised motherhood statements such as, 'Our brands are extremely valuable' would be quite insufficient to see off the Australians. What was needed was a formal brand valuation and the only company that could conduct such a valuation was Interbrand, as we were the only company that really understood brands intimately and had the skills and authority to conduct such a valuation. We ended the fax by saying that we would phone first thing on Monday morning, by which time we would be back in Britain, to organise an early meeting so that we could get on with the job of helping them defend themselves against the takeover.

A CHANCE ON A LOAF

We both knew that this was probably our best chance to gatecrash 'brand valuation', indeed, establish the entire concept and grab the market for ourselves. We had been told that a couple of the major accountancy firms (and even, it was said, McKinsey, the management consultants) had been trying for some time to develop methodologies for valuing brands, but without much success. We knew that we had to beat them to the first major high-profile brand valuation job. We also realised that a fax to RHM from Sydney, the lair of the predator GFW, would command particular attention.

We flew back to London over the weekend and on the Monday morning I called RHM.

My call was well received. I was put on to the finance director who told me that our approach to them was timely (which we knew) and that he would like to see us urgently. Accordingly, we arranged an appointment for that afternoon and Michael Birkin and I went along – Paul was tied up with another client. When we got to the meeting, we were assured of RHM's considerable interest in brand valuation and were told that the company's merchant bankers and auditors were also generally supportive, providing our methodology held water.

We were then asked to describe this methodology. In fact we did not have a closely developed, detailed procedure and I admitted this frankly, adding that this would be our first such job. However, I said that our broad approach would be to measure the projected cash flows from each brand and we would then discount each of these cash flows according to the strength of the brand. Thus, in the case of a very strong brand, one could have a high level of confidence that the cash flows would materialise, so we would apply a 'lowish' discount rate or, alternatively, a 'highish' multiple. (Discount rates or multiples are two sides of the same coin.) Conversely, a weak brand would provide much lower levels of confidence, so one would apply a higher discount rate or a lower multiple. RHM said that they thought that this was entirely logical and asked us to attend again on the Wednesday to meet their advisors. They also asked us to provide a quotation for the job of valuing their brands.

Michael and I drove out again to RHM's offices in Windsor on the Wednesday afternoon, where we met their senior finance team, the senior audit partner from their accountancy firm and two directors of their merchant bank. We described our methodology again; interest in using our services was clearly high and no one spoke out against our proposal. On the Friday we were phoned by RHM and told we had the assignment, the first ever of its kind. It was also agreed that we would meet yet again on the Monday to start work.

We were both utterly elated at the news, but also anxious. The assignment we had been awarded was momentous, but could we do it? What if we botched it? What if we ran into major technical problems? Would we have the staff to complete the job in the timescale required? Would we succeed or would we fall flat on our faces?

I can remember travelling home that evening. We had a wonderful new assignment in a totally new sector, but only a generalised idea as to how to go about it. We knew if we completed the assignment to everyone's 'satisfaction' (and RHM clearly had no doubt that we would) we would make a major impact on both marketing and accountancy, as well as business in general, and also that we would open up a huge potential new market for Interbrand; but I was consumed with anxiety.

Michael, with his accountancy background, was confident that we could apply normal auditing techniques to determine the future cash flows of each brand and that he could manage that part of the job. But how on earth were we to determine brand strength? And having determined brand strength, how would we translate this into a discount rate or multiple to apply to the brand cash flows? We agreed, accordingly, that Michael would be responsible for the brand cash flow analyses and I would spend the weekend working up a methodology to determine brand strength. We would worry later about how we combined these two analyses to arrive at a brand valuation.

THE GREY MATTER OF BRANDS

I spent most of the weekend working on the problem of how to compute brand strength at our kitchen table in Norfolk. On the way up in the car I had discussed the problem with my wife. She was involved at the time in a major epidemiological study in New York, London and Delhi, relating to mental illness in the elderly. She said that of course you can't cut open people's brains and measure the size or texture of their grey matter. You have to use questionnaires and other subjective measurements of mental function, but if these are very carefully prepared and administered, good hard data can result and this data can be comparable between, say, Delhi and New York. She said that this sort of approach was common in the medical field and she didn't see why brand strength scores, based upon questionnaires, could not be used by us.

This was reassuring, particularly as we did not have a huge team at Interbrand whom we could put in to conduct independent analyses –everyone already had a heavy workload. Also, if all the data gathering was to be done by our own people, the cost to the client would be prohibitively high. As a result,

I found the notion of brand questionnaires, completed by the client, vetted by us and then used to determine brand strength scores, very appealing.

Over the weekend I drafted a detailed brand questionnaire, which could be applied to pretty much any consumer brand. It ran to about one hundred questions and twenty pages. It specified where supporting data needed to be provided by way of appendices. I also developed a brand strength scoring system whereby, based upon the detailed information provided in the brand questionnaire, a brand strength score would be derived for each brand. I sat down and thought through the various factors that, in my view, make up a great brand and I gave each of these factors a different weight according to its importance. Thus internationality was awarded twenty five points out of a notional hundred, while legal protection was awarded five, though if the brand had no effective legal protection at all, the brand would be attributed no value whatsoever. These various scores were added up to give overall brand strength scores out of a hundred.

A hugely important international power brand such as Coca-Cola might be scored in the top eighties or early nineties, as it would score highly on every attribute, whereas a relatively weak national brand might score only in the teens or early twenties. Finally, I came up with an outline notion as to how the brand strength score could be converted into a multiple or discount rate in order to determine brand value. I did not think that there was a straight line relationship between a major world brand scoring, say, 90 on our new scale of brand strength and a 'weakish' national brand scoring say, 22 or 23. In other words, the worldwide power brand should have a multiple or discount rate well over four times greater than that of the 'weakish' national brand. I therefore proposed that the relationship between brand strength and brand value should be an S-curve, rather than a straight line, and I wrote a justification for this.

On the Monday morning Michael, Paul and I sat down together to examine the methodology we had developed between us. Over the weekend, Michael had prepared notes on how the financial audit should be conducted and he had also drafted a list of instructions for use by RHM's financial team, as they would be responsible for preparing the background numbers. We examined these together and then went through in detail the draft brand strength questionnaire, the brand strength scoring system and the valuation procedure. We all felt confident that we were on the right track. We typed up all the material and later that afternoon met with RHM's team to start the valuation.

A VERY VALUABLE MARKETING TOOL

The people assigned to the job by RHM were extremely impressive. They were bright, committed and very supportive and within four weeks had completed the detailed brand questionnaires and financial statements for over forty brands. We worked closely with them throughout and were able to solve many of the practical and methodological problems that inevitably arose as we went along. We then sat down with the data and discussed and agreed brand strength scores and, as a result, derived a valuation for each brand. In total, the valuation came to over £650 million, a staggering total, particularly at that time.

In parallel, we had commissioned one of the leading finance experts at the London Business School to examine the valuation methodology we had developed, and, in particular, the way in which we planned to combine brand profits with brand strength to derive a brand value. He advised us that that our approach was sound and this gave us great confidence.

We also started to have the first inklings that the methodology we had developed provided important and valuable insights into a company's most valuable assets, its brands. It was not at all a sterile procedure. For example, traditional accountancy procedures do not normally account on a brand-by-brand basis. They may account on a division-by-division or factory-by-factory or product line-by-product line basis but they do not normally look at individual brands or at detailed marketing, advertising and other promotional expenditures for each brand.

Similarly, it was not normal to rate brands in a detailed, incisive fashion. Views about brands tended to be developed almost in an anecdotal fashion and were not generally supported by detailed analysis. We found that our individual brand analyses cut through subjectivity and anecdote. As a result, they produced all sorts of insights into which brands could be stretched further, those which were receiving too much promotional support and should probably be placed on a care and maintenance regime and milked for profit, those which might be extended internationally, possibly through licensing arrangements, those which should be abandoned, and so forth. We started to realise, accordingly, that our brand valuation methodology was a very valuable marketing tool indeed.

During the time we were conducting the detailed programme for RHM the GFW bid fell away but the management of RHM decided that we should complete the valuation and that they would include the value derived by us on their balance sheet. No doubt the fact that there had been one unsuccessful bid already and there might yet be others played a part, as did the fact that RHM believed that the City tended to underrate the value of its brand assets. However, the most pressing immediate reason was that the company, having made a number of acquisitions in previous years and written off a great deal of goodwill against its reserves, had an apparently weak balance sheet. This could soon have triggered an accounting provision whereby relatively small transactions in the future could need shareholder approval. RHM was not concerned to evade shareholder rights; it was simply that the Stock Exchange rules could be triggered at an inappropriately low level as a result of past goodwill write-offs and this would have resulted in great inconvenience for both the company and its shareholders. In consultation with the Stock Market it was agreed that if intangible assets were included in the reserves of the company as part of the regular audit, this would be acceptable for the purposes of the Stock Market. In other words, the company's balance sheet assets could comprise both tangible and intangible assets for the purposes of this Stock Exchange test.

STUDYING THE OLD MASTERS

RHM's auditors examined the detailed valuation report and opinion prepared by Interbrand and declared themselves perfectly satisfied with it, as did the company's merchant bankers. Our valuation had a clear and justifiable audit trail and our methodology was transparent, appropriate and properly applied. All the parties gave our valuation a clean bill of health and our £650 million brand valuation was included in the company's results in 1989.

It caused a sensation. Our brand valuation and RHM's inclusion of it in their balance sheet broke entirely new ground. Though, in one or two instances in the past, intangible assets had been included in a company's balance sheet, this was always in the context of an acquisition when there was some obvious external context for the valuation. RHM's valuation of its existing brands was entirely novel; moreover it had the full support of the company's auditors and merchant bankers as well as of the Stock Exchange. It also occurred at a time when major mergers of branded goods businesses were gaining pace, leading to a growing awareness among investors of intangible brand values.

Generally the response to the valuation itself, the methodology we used and Interbrand's role was very well received indeed. For example, the '100 Group', comprising the finance directors of Britain's hundred largest companies, came out in full support and the City, too, welcomed a development which provided more data and more insights into the components of value in companies. The major audit firms, too, welcomed the move; though one or two of them said, somewhat unpleasantly, that, though they welcomed the principle of brand valuation, they did not welcome Interbrand's involvement, going on to say that brand valuation should of course be carried out by accountancy firms and not by branding consultants.

They were clearly miffed that even minor sources of income might be diverted to firms like ours. They were probably even more miffed when we responded to their sniffy comments by saying that if you were having an old master painting valued, you would ask an expert to do it, not an accountancy firm. We said that one can imagine how an accountancy firm would value such a painting. They'd probably measure its size and calculate the weight of paint on the surface of the canvas because they knew nothing about old master paintings and were simply not competent to value them. Similarly, they knew nothing about brands and should not be involved in brand valuation. This was the job of brand experts and as we were the leading branding consultancy, we were ideally placed to do the job. Our argument found much favour with most observers.

ASKING THE POPE TO TALK ABOUT ISLAM

The major opposition we encountered in those early days was from the Accounting Standards Board (ASB) and, subsequently, from certain academics at the London Business School (LBS) working as consultants to the ASB. The ASB had, in its rules, a specific provision allowing for the inclusion of intangible assets in the balance sheet. However, they had not envisaged the type of major valuation undertaken by us for RHM.

What RHM did by putting the brand valuation on its balance sheet was absolutely legitimate according to the ASB rules, but it threw the ASB into total confusion. They were a relatively slow moving organisation, which developed new accounting rules on the basis of extensive discussion and consultation. Suddenly a totally new practice had emerged that was backed by most of Britain's major companies and which was legitimate according to their own rules. However, the ASB had not anticipated formal brand valuations of the RHM/Interbrand kind and their immediate response was to try to put the whole thing on hold for a few years until they had talked it through and formed a view as to whether it was a good or a bad thing. They were not necessarily hostile to our valuation; they just wanted a few years to think things through.

Consequently, the ASB issued a formal request to companies asking them to hold off for a while so that they could consider the whole business of intangible assets and how they should be treated on balance sheets. Fortunately for us, companies were in no mood to listen and pressed ahead with brand valuations with enthusiasm, mostly using Interbrand.

The ASB responded to this by asking London Business School to conduct an 'independent' study of balance sheet valuations in general and, in particular, the inclusion of intangibles. LBS's academics working in this area were widely known to have an almost religious belief in the 'sanctity' of the balance sheet. They had argued that balance sheets were simply that: a means of balancing the cash coming into and out of a business. They argued that items on a balance sheet should never be revalued and that the purpose of a balance sheet was not to show the underlying strength or worth of a business but simply to balance its cash flows. Thus if a building was bought for £1,000 in 1850 and was now worth £1 million, this was no concern for the balance sheet. The original figure should appear on the balance sheet less a figure for depreciation. They also argued that intangible assets should never appear on balance sheets, except, perhaps, in the context of an acquisition, though this was debatable.

It was therefore clear to everyone that, by asking the LBS to conduct an 'independent' review, the ASB were shopping for the opinion they wanted. Having failed to stop brand valuation themselves, they were looking for an authority to support their case. We said to journalists, when asked, that for the ASB to ask the LBS to give an impartial view of brand valuation was about as absurd as asking the Pope to give an impartial view of Islam. Nonetheless any critical pronouncements by the LBS team would, we knew, be widely reported and could have a serious effect on our new brand valuation activities. We therefore had a serious problem. It was clear to us that LBS was really looking forward to giving brand valuation, and Interbrand, a bloody nose.

LBS's view was that they had no great objection in principle to brand valuation or to our methodology – in fact, they broadly approved – but they could not condone what was being done to the balance sheet by us and our clients. We were equally certain that they were wrong, They were taking an absurdly narrow view of the balance sheet as the balance sheet in modern businesses played an entirely different role from that of a generation or two earlier. Companies and investors talked about balance sheet strength and expected a company's balance sheet to reflect its worth. LBS's view was, we thought, out-dated.

ACADEMICS IN SANDALS

Having conducted their review, a major public meeting was called by the LBS at which their academics would deliver their verdict. Dozens of financial journalists were invited to attend. We contacted the LBS to ask if we could attend too. This request was clearly perceived by them as being like Beelzebub asking to attend the College of Cardinals in Rome. We were told in no uncertain terms that we would not be welcome and, as we did not have the nerve to defy them, we had no choice but to skulk in our offices. Around mid-morning of the day in question, we began to receive a series of phone calls from financial journalists who had slipped out of the meeting to hear Interbrand's response to LBS's pronouncements. They all told us the same story: LBS had tried to rubbish brand valuation for balance sheet purposes. We were told that there was a pervasive air of triumphalism and we were clearly seen by LBS as the ones who had been vanquished.

One journalist, from *The Times Business News*, asked me what I thought our brand valuation clients would make of LBS's forceful views. I replied, somewhat optimistically, that I did not think that they would be too worried by the opinions of a bunch of academics in sandals. I said this jokingly, and did not think I would be quoted, but I was not worried if I was because, from our and our clients' point of view, scuppering the LBS study was critically important. And in any case, we were irritated at their treatment of us, so felt they were fair game.

The next morning *The Times* ran a leader in its Business section on the

LBS study and my mischievous comment was repeated. The term 'academics in sandals' became widely quoted and hugely upset the authors of the LBS report. The effect of the amused coverage was that LBS's report and recommendations were totally ignored and the ASB's request to companies to 'go easy' was utterly disregarded too. Brand valuation roared ahead once more and we had come out on top, partly due to one tongue-in-cheek comment.

For at least a couple of years thereafter, we suffered a considerable frostiness from the LBS academics. Several of them refused to sit on a platform with anyone from Interbrand; it was clear that they felt that my comment was a punch below the belt. Perhaps it was, but it was, I was sure, a scrap that they had largely initiated. Then I had an appointment to meet someone at LBS, not one of those involved in the brand valuation controversy, on a completely different matter.

I was waiting in the reception area at the Business School when one of the principal authors of the earlier report, who was particularly wounded by my remark to *The Times*, walked in. He saw me, recognised my face, but did not immediately remember who I was. He walked towards me, put out his hand and, suddenly, the penny dropped. He muttered something under his breath and looked down at his feet. I looked too: he was wearing sandals. He was mortified beyond belief, but after a few moments saw the funny side of it. Later, friendly relations were resumed.

A BRAND AUTHORITY

Brand valuation developed over the years into a hugely important business activity for Interbrand. It provided an entirely new income stream and also gave us enormous exposure in the financial press and elsewhere, as well as great authority in the world of marketing. We were also able to develop and refine our methodology and found a host of new applications for it.

For example, even though most of our early projects involved financial accounts and the balance sheet, such applications quickly became only a minor part of our brand valuation business. We used our methodology to help companies defend themselves against takeover, to evaluate acquisition candidates in conjunction with merchant banks, to justify brand licensing arrangements to tax authorities, for brand management and brand monitoring purposes and to help companies develop overall brand and corporate strategies. We found ourselves working with companies at the highest possible level and being involved in some of the most profound business decisions companies were confronted with. Brand valuation – for various applications – also became a worldwide business. Soon we were undertaking major assignments in the US, Sweden, Japan, India, indeed everywhere and anywhere. The notion that brands had value and this value is measurable struck a chord with businesses worldwide.

Interbrand thus became a familiar name to bankers, investors, financial journalists and senior managers. Single-handedly we were instrumental, I believe, in transforming how brands and branding are viewed by the business world. From being mere wordsmiths, we had now made branding and marketing central to the business agenda. In particular, marketing efforts and expenditure increasingly came to be seen as investments just like any other, but investments in intangible assets, in brands, not in tangible assets.

I am quite sure that observers looking back will see this as one of the most remarkable changes in business thinking for many years. The underlying forces, whereby intangibles were coming to play a more important role in business decision making, were at work anyway, but Interbrand helped crystallise what was happening and bring it to the attention of important audiences.

In the mid 80s we had described the process of branding, but it was brand valuation that electrified business in general and the world of marketing and advertising in particular. Now the fact that brands have value is a concept that is utterly familiar to everyone, even to every teenager in the world, or so it would seem.

Curiously, two of the audiences who came to benefit most from this changing culture took almost no notice of what was happening for several years. The first was trade mark lawyers who did not seem to think that brand valuation would have any real effect on their world – it was a marketing phenomenon which largely passed them by. In fact, it brought to the attention of companies that trade mark lawyers looked after their most valuable assets and thus that they were much more important members of the team than they had been considered hitherto. Trade mark lawyers, previously forgotten members of the legal profession and of the world of commerce, suddenly became more central and valued.

The second group to largely ignore brand valuation and the branding revolution at the outset was advertising agencies. The effect of brand valuation was, as I have mentioned, to persuade brand owners to view marketing and, in particular, advertising expenditure as an investment, not a necessary but lost expense. Viewed in this light, advertising potentially assumes a much more important role in a company's affairs, as the term 'investing' in a brand shows, but advertising agencies failed to recognise this and generally treated the brand valuation debate, if they noticed it at all, as something peripheral and of no concern to them. It took them years to change and now they seem to believe they came up with it all in the first place.

Brand valuation raised the profile of Interbrand, and branding, globally. Above all, it continued our tradition of providing differentiated, innovative, technical services to our clients. It would provide us with valuable and sustainable revenues and enhance our reputation for years to come... or so we thought.

11

THE GOLDEN YEARS – MOSTLY

In which we learnt the importance of a ruthless focus on quality and a restless desire for innovation to build a great business.

Though I say it myself, Interbrand was, in the late 1980s and early 1990s, a quite exceptional company with terrific people, the best products around, enormous innovative ability, great esprit de corps and a truly international reach.

Our Head Office in London remained the ideas centre with most of our new products and methodologies originating there. Staff numbers grew to about eighty in our splendid new offices, located directly above Covent Garden tube station, and our team included linguists, creatives, accountants, trade mark attorneys, graphic designers, strategists and marketing experts. On many assignments all of these skills would be brought to bear, with everyone working together seamlessly. We did not allow 'nesting' or the development of separate small empires. All of us worked for the same company and we were all passionate about branding, about doing the finest possible work and about satisfying the needs of our clients.

I don't think any of us were particularly precious or arrogant, but we prided ourselves on never losing an assignment to a so-called competitor. We felt that branding was ours, that we had been the first to recognise and describe it, in other words, to 'codify' it. We believed we knew more about branding than anyone else and were damned if anybody was going to beat us to a job. Fortunately, this never involved price-cutting; in fact, the reverse. I mentioned earlier how several of the design companies we had worked with decided that naming was a lucrative business and had set up in competition with us usually by offering a cut price service. Another entrant into the naming market at that time was the largest trade mark law practice in Britain which, though they publicly purported to look down on marketing activities, set up their own consultancy.

CHEAP HEART BYPASS, ANYONE?

We were therefore not surprised when, once brand valuation broke, many competitors emerged, including the accountancy firms. All decided, it seemed, that the way to compete with Interbrand was to offer their services at a substantially lower price than us. In our early days, we had earnest discussions about how best to meet cut-price competition in the product naming area. I had argued then that the cost of a name, in relation to the overall cost of launching a new product, was relatively modest and I could not see anyone economising on the name by going for the lowest quote. It would be as daft as buying a cheap heart bypass operation. We therefore maintained our prices and after a few months increased them substantially. We realised time after time that our arriviste competitors were quoting such extraordinarily low prices compared with us, that it did not so much make us look expensive as them look absurdly, unbelievably cheap. I cannot recall losing a single assignment on the grounds of price and our margins rose appreciably. We maintained this policy of 'full but fair' pricing throughout my time at Interbrand for all the services we offered including brand valuation – though we always offered the assurance of 'satisfaction or your blockage back'.

In the field of brand valuation, the most aggressive competition came from the major accountancy practices. In the early days, as I have mentioned, they were all pretty sniffy about the concept and particularly about our methodology, but within months virtually every one had set up its own brand valuation department trumpeting a new, improved methodology. In fact, all such methodologies proved to be merely our methodology with one or two minor tweaks, not one of which was a true improvement. The reason they were able to get hold of our methodology so quickly was that the valuation work we carried out for RHM and, subsequently, many other major companies had to be completely transparent and verifiable and it was the major audit firms who were doing the verifying by auditing our valuations. We had, in effect, to train potential competitors in our procedures and they were not slow to copy us. However, even though they had inside access to our methods, they did not know anything about brands or branding and from what we saw of it, their work was never of a high quality. But they were able to win a few projects.

We also realised that, as our methodology had to be so transparent we might as well open it up completely if only to ensure a standardisation of brand valuation techniques. We therefore published *Brand Valuation*, an edited work, and this threw open our approach to all. This book proved popular, we are told, among our competitors and for several years, key chapters were the most photocopied works in British business schools.

A BIT OF SPORT

One example of how the major accountancy practices won clients came to our attention a year or so after the RHM brand valuation assignment. We were asked to pitch for a major balance sheet valuation by the British subsidiary of a large Scandinavian business. A day or two later they called to say that we had been successful and would we start work immediately, as the valuation was a matter of some urgency? This we did. But then a couple of days further on, their finance director phoned to say that we were to stop work at once as they had no choice but to take the work away from us and give it to their auditors. He explained that, as well as Interbrand, he had asked the firm's auditors to pitch for doing the valuation work. He said that they had put up a pretty pathetic show but later, when he told them that they had not got the job, they had said that if the valuation was done by us they, the auditors, might not be able to give the company's accounts a clean audit certificate and the company's financial reporting process might be seriously compromised. If, on the other hand, the company was to cancel the Interbrand work and give it to the auditors' own brand valuation team, there should be no problems with the audit certificate, nor should there be any delay in completing the audit. Our client was desperately embarrassed but said that under the circumstances he had no choice but to agree to the accounting firm's 'suggestions'.

We knew of other instances where similar tactics had been employed but not as blatantly as this. We were furious and considered various strategies to right what we considered an appalling injustice. Finally, I rang Sir Patrick Sergeant, an eminent business journalist and editor. I told him the story, but did not mention the name of the auditors or of the client. The next morning he ran a thunderous leader describing how we had been cheated out of work. Immediately, stuff started hitting the fan. Our client rang us to say that, even though no one had been named, the auditors knew that it was them in the frame and they were worried stiff. However, he could now switch the work back to Interbrand without any fear of reprisals, and this he did.

Later that same day, the senior partner at the accountancy firm in question phoned me. He was obviously terrified that their name would come out and his initial strategy was to bluster and attack. He told me that what we had done was a disgrace and no professional should ever give such a story to a major newspaper. He said I ought to be ashamed of myself; I was neither an officer nor a gentleman. I pointed out to him that I had not mentioned his firm's name and he should be grateful for this. Indeed, it was his firm that needed to hang its head in shame. If he continued to attack me, I added, I would get on the phone immediately to Sir Patrick and give him this further nugget of information. He immediately started to beg me not to do so and apologised repeatedly for the behaviour of his firm. He said it would never happen again but of course it happened all the time.

I never understood how auditors were (and still are) allowed to offer non-audit services to their clients, nor why firms were not required by law to change their auditors every few years. The cosy arrangement in Britain and elsewhere whereby auditors offered additional services to clients that could be worth several times more than the not inconsiderable audit fee, and where auditors formed lucrative relationships with clients extending over decades, was a licence for corruption, albeit a gentlemanly form thereof.

We rather enjoyed our run-ins with 'authority' and took pleasure in being somewhat irreverent and iconoclastic. I don't think we were particularly difficult or ever looked for a fight, but neither were we a pushover. In Ireland the term for our behaviour was 'enjoying a bit of craic'; at Interbrand we used to refer to it as having 'a bit of sport'. Everyone in the firm enjoyed the fun and it was an important factor in binding us all together.

WHY DO YOU WEAR A TIE?

Another such run-in involved a director of the then Midland Bank. We had had an enquiry from Hong Kong and Shanghai Bank (HSBC) in Hong Kong and I stopped off to meet them on a trip to Sydney. We had an agreeable discussion in their beautiful offices overlooking the Hong Kong waterfront. They explained that they had recently acquired Britain's Midland Bank and needed to consider whether to keep this name, brand their UK business 'HSBC' or choose and use a new name altogether. They were particularly concerned that if they went the HSBC route, their full title – The Hong Kong and Shanghai Banking Corporation – would, when used, prove rather too complex and exotic for the average British man, or woman, in the street. They asked that we quote for an exploratory study to examine the strategic options and also include some potential new names for the business. Perhaps, they said, they might adopt one of these in conjunction with their existing distinctive logo and livery. My response was that I, too, felt the Midland brand was pretty tarnished, but if I was them I would not adopt a new name, I'd simply re-name the acquired business HSBC in conjunction with their familiar corporate identity. I said that they would rarely need to use their name in full except, perhaps, on legal documents; and when they did, I couldn't foresee any problems. Besides, no one knew what the initials BMW stood for and if BMW worked in the UK, why not HSBC? I said they really had no need of branding advisors like us, as the solution was so straightforward!

They replied that this solution had, of course, occurred to them already and it was most probable that they would go this route, but, for thoroughness, they would like Interbrand to conduct an exercise reviewing alternative strategies and possible new names. These latter suggestions should include existing names belonging to members of the group as well as entirely new names. (Later I came to realise that HSBC was doing this to keep the directors of Midland Bank 'sweet' – they wanted to show that they were not, unthinkingly, imposing the name HSBC on them.)

I returned to London and we prepared our strategy recommendations. We then, as required, went on to conduct creative work using researchers, copywriters and creative groups. It was not, in truth, a particularly onerous assignment, as it seemed clear that the only sensible route was to adopt the HSBC name. So the whole process seemed something of a waste of effort. Then, later, when I phoned Hong Kong to fix a date to present our ideas they asked that, in the first instance, we present our work, and in particular the new names, to a director of Midland Bank in London and his team.

Paul Stobart and I made the presentation. At that time, our presentation method was an overhead projector and acetates. Computer graphics were in their infancy and the proposed names were drawn onto the acetates by a computer-controlled pen, known to us as 'the palsied hand' because the machine laboriously drew each name in a jerky, apparently uncertain fashion. When we arrived at Midland Bank's head office in the City we met a very frosty reception and I soon realised we were in for an unpleasant encounter. I started the presentation to the director and four or five of his senior marketing team by explaining how I had gone to Hong Kong, met the HSBC people and been given an assignment.

The Midland Bank director interrupted me to say, in an angry and aggressive way, that I should not have gone to Hong Kong without his permission; how dare I go over his head. I said I didn't even know he existed until a few days earlier and certainly didn't need his permission to visit his superiors. He grumbled and said no more. A little later I put an introductory acetate onto the projector screen. It simply read something along the lines of, 'Branding Proposals prepared for Midland Bank Group plc'. I had been asked to go along with the fiction that Midland bank was our client, not HSBC.

As soon as this slide went up the director became red in the face and screamed, "You're a naming company, aren't you?" I said we were and he then said, "Well, the least you could bloody well do is get our bloody name right." I asked him what was wrong and he told me that I was so damned sloppy I'd even got the wrong name on the first slide. I was baffled and angry, but a little bit concerned that perhaps he might be right.

I quickly passed the presentation over to Paul and surreptitiously located the file in my briefcase. I then compared the name on my slide with that on the front page of Midland Bank's Annual Report and Accounts. I had got their name precisely correct. I was furious. I stopped the meeting and said that I had just been sworn and shouted at and accused of incompetence, but I had now checked the name we had used on the slide and I had been right all along; it was him who had made the mistake and I thought he ought to apologise to me for his unpleasant behaviour. He blustered and said that it was the name on the Annual Report that was incorrect and the corporate affairs people were always making silly bloody mistakes! He refused to apologise saying that he was not prepared to discuss the matter any further. "Get on with your bloody presentation," he said.

A few moments later, he interrupted the meeting again. He looked at the name suggestions we were presenting and said, "Who designed these?" At first I didn't know what he was talking about, but then it dawned on me that he was referring to the typeface we had chosen. He wouldn't let me answer his question and launched into a shrieking attack – "We have paid you for bloody names, not for bloody design. I'll speak to my people in Hong Kong and tell them to reduce your bill as we're not prepared to pay you for bloody design work," and so forth. He seemed to lose all control (the f-word was also well used) and my attempts at reasoning with him were hopeless. He kept asking why we had used a fancy design for the proposed names in our presentation and insisting that 'he' was not prepared to pay for our design work. I said we had chosen the typeface simply because it looked attractive and for no other reason. There was no cost whatsoever to them for this. We had simply selected one of the typefaces available on our computer. Nonetheless he continued to shout and swear at me.

Finally, I lost my temper. I asked him why he wore a tie and then said, "I know why you wear a tie; it's because it bloody well looks better. You don't use it to wipe your nose. You don't use it to hold up your bloody trousers. You don't use it to clean your bloody desk. You wear it because it bloody well looks better and that's why I chose that bloody typeface." I was ready for a good row, but secretly was having a smashing time. We faced each other, glowering and red-faced.

Suddenly Paul Stobart, who had seemed anxious when I first launched into my tirade, cracked. He roared with laughter and almost fell off his chair. The Midland Bank people cracked too though they were obviously fearful of showing too much mirth at the expense of their silly and irascible boss. I too got the giggles and a difficult moment was over. The rest of the presentation went well. When we returned to the office, Paul and I were still laughing as we walked through reception. We must have made a noisy entrance as virtually the entire office turned out to hear about the latest bit of sport. Afterwards we realised that the bad temper displayed by this man was almost certainly due to his resentment at Midland Bank's being taken over by HSBC. He probably suspected he might soon lose his job (he did) and we were convenient whipping boys. Clearly, the knowledge that he would most likely leave with a large cheque in his pocket and a juicy pension was insufficient consolation.

DAVID MEETS GOLIATH

One of my pet business hates is those companies, fortunately quite few in number, who routinely seem to bully their suppliers. During my years at

Interbrand, I must have worked for hundreds of clients in at least a couple of dozen countries and I remember almost all of them with great affection. Unfortunately a small minority tend to lodge in one's mind and I must tell you of one in particular.

British Oxygen Company (BOC) was not, in fact, strictly an Interbrand client, but the head of their intellectual property department had been friendly with our trade mark attorneys for years and I got to know him quite well as he liked our Christmas parties and always ensured he got an invitation.

One day a friend phoned me to say that he had seen one of our new trucks and to congratulate me on our new venture. I was completely bemused and said there must be a mistake, as we had no trucks. Over the next couple of weeks, several more people mentioned that they'd seen trucks with our name on them. Then, looking out of my office in Covent Garden one day, I saw a huge forty-foot monster driving down Long Acre with the name 'BOC Interbrand' emblazoned on the side. Interbrand was shown in red, the same as on our letterhead, and the typestyle was very similar to ours; the initials BOC were not particularly prominent. It later transpired that BOC Interbrand was a new distribution arm of BOC, specialising in the distribution of branded goods.

I wrote to the head of intellectual property at BOC, whom I knew quite well, to ask him what was going on and to express my concern. A few days later, I received back from him a formal 'Dear Mr Murphy' letter saying, in effect, that if I didn't like it, I could sue. I wrote back that, as branding specialists, it was extremely embarrassing to find our name being used by someone else and we had to take the matter very seriously. I also said that I was surprised that he had not advised his people of our existence, as he knew us so well. Why did he let his company take our name?

The argument continued, but after several weeks I had got nowhere and decided it was time to light the blue touch paper. I asked one of my team to go to Companies House to get the home address details of all BOC's directors. One Friday afternoon, I posted a Recorded Delivery package to each director in which I set out the problem and my sense of grievance. It went to all of their home addresses. I also attached copies of the correspondence. The reason I sent these letters on a Friday afternoon was that I wanted the recipients, both executive and non-executive, to have to climb out of bed on a Saturday morning, put on their dressing gowns and go down to sign for the post. I then wanted them to have all weekend to mull over what I had said. I knew that by the Monday morning, things would become lively and I was right.

Unfortunately, BOC still refused to settle and the correspondence became increasingly heated. We had a meeting with their company secretary to try to resolve matters but he too refused to budge. Their position was that they had invested millions of pounds in the liveries of a large fleet of trucks and they weren't about to change. If we cared to, we could sue them, but they had much deeper pockets than we did and it was cheaper for them to defend a legal action than to repaint all their trucks, warehouses and so forth. I replied that I knew that suing them would probably cost Interbrand a minimum of £500,000, that it would tie up me and my senior management team for months and, as ever with the law, the outcome was uncertain. But I was not an idiot and did not plan to sue them, as there was another route we could take that would cost nothing and was bound to succeed. They said to do whatever I wanted as they would not back down. They clearly didn't believe we could possibly win.

I bought £1,000 worth of BOC shares and registered them in the names of various directors and senior colleagues as well as my own. A few days before BOC's Annual General Meeting at the Savoy Hotel I called the company secretary of BOC to tell him that I would attend the AGM as a shareholder and would be asking some questions. I started at this point to detect the first notes of anxiety. Before the meeting, eight of us gathered in the boardroom at our offices in Covent Garden and I distributed a series of pre-prepared questions. We all then set off for the Savoy, only a few hundred yards away. We each registered separately and sat in different parts of the meeting hall. I was the last to arrive and, before sitting down, went to the lavatory. I was standing washing my hands when I heard two heavies, one on each side, mention my name. I didn't say a word, but knew that we were in for a lively meeting.

I took my seat in the fourth row, just by the centre aisle. The chairman of BOC, Richard Giordano, an American, and the rest of the BOC board sat on a dais about six feet higher than the audience of four or five hundred people. Shortly after I sat down, Giordano turned to the company secretary and said, in his American accent, "Point out that guy, Murphy, to me." They both peered deep into the hall and didn't see me immediately below them, so I stood up and introduced myself. They both looked hugely discomfited.

The first item on the agenda was the audit report and it was presented by the senior audit partner of the then Coopers & Lybrand. He said that he was proud to present the company's accounts and that they were the twenty-fifth set of accounts that his firm had prepared for BOC. Afterwards Giordano asked if there were any questions. I put up my hand to enquire what the audit fee was – I was told it was £1.25 million, a very substantial sum, at the time. I next asked if the audit firm provided other services to BOC and the chairman eventually responded, clearly quite reluctantly, that Coopers & Lybrand had undertaken consulting work in the previous year, amounting to several more millions; in other words, the firm's consulting income from BOC was several times that of its – not inconsiderable – audit income.

I said that I thought that it was potentially corrupting for an audit firm to carry out non-audit work, as it was all too easy to nod through a questionable item if an undertaking had been given by the clients that the auditors will be paid an additional fee to fix the problem. I said I was not suggesting that this had happened, but as one of the owners of the business (about a dozen shares were registered in my name), I would like any possibility of its happening to be removed. I would, accordingly, like the audit firm to be restricted solely to auditing. I went on to say that I also required the auditors to serve for no more than five years at a stretch. I thought for a company to have the same auditors for twenty-five years was way, way too cosy, particularly considering the huge fees involved.

By now the chairman was becoming agitated, even though he knew that the firm would win any vote as it held all the voting proxies of its institutional investors. (These seldom bother to attend routine AGMs.) So, even if every small shareholder in the room voted with me, we would still speak for only a small minority of the votes. When my proposals were put to the vote, a few shareholders supported me, but most didn't and my proposals were voted down.

We then got on to directors' salaries. Giordano was well known in the City as the man who did more than any other to boost the pay packets of directors of British businesses; his salary and those of his colleagues seemed to me to be inappropriately high. Not only that, they had all taken large bonuses and stock options in a year when the company had not done particularly well. I therefore had great fun laying into the board about their salaries. This time I received a little more support from my fellow small shareholders. I detected a little more unease on the part of the Board, but the proxy votes won the day yet again.

The next issue was the retirement age of a non-executive director, another American. He was over seventy-five and wished to remain on the board, I suspect because he enjoyed his non-executive director's fees. Directors could only remain after seventy-five with the approval of shareholders. I asked what the compulsory retirement age was for BOC staff and was told it was normally sixty, though in exceptional cases, people could stay on to sixty-five. I asked why, if the company did not think an executive should serve beyond sixty-five, a director could serve beyond seventy-five? Wasn't this illogical and absurd? Another row broke out with the director in question offering to race me along the Strand. We lost that vote too, but we were now getting into our stride.

I then distributed photographs of one of BOC Interbrand's trucks and launched into a passionate denouncement of the way in which my company had been treated. I raised this issue when the subject of business ethics had been mentioned by the chairman, asking him if BOC had ethical guidelines for its directors and staff and, if so, why they thought it ethical to take my company's name. By this time, the meeting was descending into chaos. Groups of security people were starting to gather on either side of the hall near to where I sat. I had been polite and objective and there was no reason why anyone should be entitled to throw me out, but the board was beginning to lose it and I was starting to tire.

At this point I threw the baton to my colleagues and the fun continued. Janet Fogg stood up and asked what the company's policy was on the employment of women and, in particular, why the company had an all-male board. They had no suitable answer.

Another colleague, Tom Blackett, asked what measures the company had prepared in the event a hostile bidder appeared. He said that Lord Hanson had built up a stake in ICI and, fearing a bid, ICI had hived off its pharmaceutical division as Zeneca. Did BOC have any similar strategy in place? Members of the BOC board had no idea that all the people asking these impertinent questions were Interbranders and Tom's question completely threw them. Giordano blustered and then said that there was a plan to sell off the medical gases division, should a predator appear. This was an absolutely plum piece of information and it was very indiscreet of him to publicly disclose it, but, fortunately for him, no member of the financial press was there to report it. Nor was the answer of much interest to us as we were simply there to create mayhem.

Questions went on and on and a few of the other shareholders became emboldened by our stance and started to ask difficult questions of their own. The BOC board clearly had its worst ever AGM. We totally wrecked it, but we did so in a legal and polite way.

After the AGM the CEO, yet another American, approached me and asked if he could have a private word. We went to a quiet corner of the room and his first question was, "Why are you doing this to us?" I said that there were really three main reasons. First, as the world's leading branding and identity consultancy, our name was very important to us and we could not let them take it. Second, I bitterly resented getting an unpleasant 'Dear Mr Murphy' letter from their intellectual property lawyer who was so well known to me. And the third reason was that I really enjoyed it.

He gulped, particularly at the last reason, and said that they wished to settle with us. I replied that it was best if they did, as I would take pleasure in wrecking every shareholder meeting they held until I got my way. A few days later, he sent his car for me and we had lunch in his office. He pointed to a tall stack of papers on the side of the desk. He told me that these were all the papers on the dispute and he had spent more time over the previous six months on this single matter than on any other. I said he should have settled earlier and he agreed. We reached a deal that they would change the name of their division within three months and remove the name BOC Interbrand from all their trucks within twelve months. Later, we heard that BOC had thirty lawyers at the AGM, as well as a sound recording crew and a team of 'heavies', two of whom I had seen in the lavatory before the meeting. Our tactics caused them serious anxiety. For us, it was mainly good fun, though with a deadly serious purpose.

12

THE NIGHT OF THE LONG KNIVES

*In which we became book publishers, feasted on giant king
tuna in Japan, and narrowly escaped a financial crisis.*

THE BOOK OF BRANDS

Besides developing our business on all fronts, over this period we also
produced a number of new books designed to reinforce our position as
leaders in the emerging field of branding. One was an edited work called
Brand Valuation, which, as I mentioned earlier, was designed to help make
brand valuation 'ours', or at least in large part ours. In order to reinforce
our emerging position in the field of design, we wrote *How To Design Trade
marks and Logos,* a how-to-do-it textbook, which proved very popular
among design students, particularly in the US. I also wrote *Brand Strategy*
to develop certain themes first covered in *Branding – A Key Marketing Tool.*
Our most popular book, however, proved to be *The World's Greatest Brands,*
published in 1989.

For years we had planned to produce a glossy group-wide brochure
setting out our work, our clients, our offices, our capabilities and our
philosophy. Every time we had a board meeting or a group conference
the matter would come up and we would delegate one office or another to
prepare the design of the new brochure on behalf of the entire group. Each
group company would simply have to translate the text and drop in its own
illustrations. Unfortunately if the New York office came up with proposals,
the London office would reject them; whatever London came up with, New
York hated; and Tokyo's suggestions were never approved by anybody. I
found the subject of the group brochure entirely disheartening – the subject
recurred time and time again but was never resolved. Suddenly I had an
idea. Why not prepare a glossy coffee table book on brands that we could

give to clients as a quasi-brochure and also sell through book sellers? It would be a much less expensive solution – the estimates we had received for printing the group brochure were toe-curling – and it would also command more authority. I also saw it as a way of infiltrating ourselves into a client's consciousness without making a hard sell. And I doubted that any client would toss an attractive book in the bin, the fate of most fancy brochures.

This new approach to the brochure problem was agreed by everyone. We decided to feature in our new book what we considered to be the world's 300 greatest brands. These would be selected by us and divided into world brands and regional brands. These brands would also be organised by product sector and would be scored and ranked using our new brand evaluation methodology. Finally we would include chapters on the importance of branding and on the rules of good brand management. All of us thought this was a great initiative, but, as ever, no one wanted the job of editing the new book, so it reluctantly fell to me. I prepared an outline of the book and divided up the work of compiling descriptions of the 300 chosen brands among colleagues. About a dozen people had each to contact about twenty-five brand owners and prepare short synopses of the chosen brand. They also had to put together photographs and other illustrations.

I should have known better. Terry Oliver in Japan, David Andrew in Sydney and Paul Stobart in London did what was asked of them promptly and to a high standard, as did certain other colleagues, but many did not – they were too busy they said! I found the publication deadline we had set ourselves drawing ever closer with much of the organising and drafting still to be done.

WHAT THE HELL SHALL WE DO?

I realised that the only way the book would ever be finished was for me to do more of it. The problem was that this was pre-internet and pre-Google, so digging out information on brands was not always too easy. We decided that the best approach was simply to write to companies, describe what we were doing and ask them for the information we required and for suitable illustrations. We would explain that it was an honour for the company's brand or brands to be included in our splendid new book and of course there would be no charge. Most companies proved only too happy to help.

McDonald's, for example, sent a fantastic information pack almost by return and Tabasco did the same, together with a huge box of samples.

Kimberly Clark, on the other hand, was not at all helpful. We had asked for non-confidential background information on the Kleenex and Kotex brands, all of which was in the public domain. We didn't hear anything for a while and, when we sent a reminder to them in Wisconsin, we received a fax from a woman vice president saying, in effect, that if we dared to include their brands in our wretched new book, we would face legal action. We had almost finished the book by this time and really wanted to include these two brands. The solution we found was to write across the bottom of the fax a message, ostensibly to me, which read, 'John, if Joe Blow [the president of KC, whose name we had looked up in a directory] hears about this, he will be furious, given his support for the book when you told him about it at that conference. What the hell shall we do?' We then 'inadvertently' sent the fax back to the woman who had sent us the original. We had clearly made a terrible, but not uncommon, 'mistake'. Within a couple of days we received a further fax saying that unfortunately an error had occurred earlier and the information we had requested was being couriered to us that very day.

When the book came out it was an immediate success. We published it ourselves in the UK with a print run of 10,000 copies, most of which were sold through the book trade. Complimentary copies were however sent by us to clients and prospective clients, of course. In the US, rights to the book were taken up by a major publisher and sales in that market rose to over 50,000 copies. The book also did well in other overseas markets. But probably the major impact of the book was to encourage us to produce an annual league table of the world's most powerful and valuable brands. This was taken up first by the *Financial Times* and subsequently by *Business Week*. Now Interbrand's various brand valuation rankings receive enormous exposure and generate huge interest. Indeed, it is probably the most potent tool in the branding industry. Another effect of the book was to challenge existing perceptions; for example, we included the BBC as one of Britain's greatest brands. The BBC was astounded at this as no one within the corporation had previously ever thought of the BBC as being remotely 'a brand'. I am told that our inclusion of the BBC caused huge debate within the corporation and marked the start of a major change in the BBC's strategy and culture.

'YOU GOTTA CHARGE TOP DOLLAR'

Interbrand's London office serviced clients in the UK, Scandinavia and the Netherlands and provided technical assistance worldwide on brand valuation projects. The UK business grew strongly and made great profits but its performance was matched and often exceeded by that of the US business. You may recall that I first met Chuck Brymer, a twenty-seven-year-old recent recruit, when I turned up at the US office in the middle of a hurricane to deal with a serious staff problem. Chuck quickly and efficiently got that business under control and, before I left to return to London, asked that he be considered for the role of president of Interbrand US. I had been extremely impressed by him in the short time I had known him but felt that such an appointment might be a little premature, though I knew that American businesses had a great respect for youth, as did I. I compromised, therefore, and told Chuck that I would hold off looking to make a new appointment for three months. If he did the sort of job I thought he could, then the job would then be his on a permanent basis. He accepted the challenge and from that day on Interbrand US blossomed under Chuck's leadership.

Within five years we had opened branch offices in Chicago and San Francisco and were offering a full range of services – name creation (but not trade mark law), packaging design, corporate identity design, brand strategy, market research and brand valuation, the latter with technical support from London. We thought that the prices we charged at the London business were pretty fancy at times, but they were eclipsed by those of the US office. Chuck's view, and he proved to be correct, was that top quality implied high fees: 'You gotta charge top dollar'.

The culture in the US business was, however, somewhat different from that of the UK. Every time I visited the New York office there were new faces and staff members who, a month earlier, had told me earnestly that working for Interbrand was the most exciting thing they had ever done in their entire lives, had resigned and left for a new, even more exciting challenge. I also found that the US business was more than happy for new products and methodologies to be crafted in the UK and then passed to them. The emphasis was very much on 'the sale'. Frequently I would be asked, 'What new products have you got for us?' The team in the US loved to have a constant stream of new ideas come over from London and they proved more than capable of honing and adapting these to suit the American market.

Over the years I came to greatly appreciate Chuck Brymer; he has a fantastic sense of humour, enormous energy, great personal charisma and excellent business skills. He also took to the Interbrand culture like a natural and built a US business that was head and shoulders above all its competitors. He would in due course become Group CEO; and better still, in 2006, he was appointed the worldwide head of DDB, one of the world's largest advertising agencies and part of the Omnicom empire.

RENAMING TOYO WHALERS

If we were delighted by how our businesses performed in the UK and USA, we were equally proud of how we were doing in Japan. Japan was considered by most western marketing services businesses with operations there to be a graveyard of hopes. Almost no such western business operating in the Japanese market made money and most made extraordinarily huge losses by the time they paid their expat managers, provided them with western-style apartments and met their restaurant and entertainment bills. In the advertising and marketing services sector it was a fact, I was assured, that for years not a single Japanese subsidiary of a major western business had made a single yen of profit. Most, of course, did not even think of making a profit – advertising agencies, for example, set up subsidiaries in Tokyo so that it looked good on their notepaper and in order to appear to be able to handle international accounts. Almost none did any work whatsoever for Japanese businesses, only for those western clients who wanted to advertise in Japan. Interbrand Japan, therefore, under the leadership of Terry Oliver, was a shining exception to the rule as it was highly successful, very profitable, and worked largely for major Japanese businesses.

Terry Oliver was a Londoner who started work as a journalist and first visited Japan when, in his twenties, he decided to tour the world. He loved the country and the culture and lived in Japan for the rest of his working life. He spoke and wrote perfect Japanese and was the ideal manager. He joined us, as I have mentioned, when he and Harada-san were assigned to the joint venture business by our new Japanese partners. A few years later our partners offered to sell us their 50% share in the business and we accepted gratefully. Interbrand Japan worked on naming, packaging, corporate identity, valuation and strategy assignments for all the major Japanese businesses including Toyota, Nissan, Shiseido, Fuji Film, Matsushita and Sony, as well as for western incomers such as Coca-Cola and Nestlé.

I was sometimes required to fly over for a guest appearance, as the role of chairman is extremely important in Japan. For me this was always a wonderful treat. I could enjoy a trip to one of the most interesting and exciting countries in the world, but was required to do nothing on arrival except bow and smile. I couldn't understand a word that was being said in the meetings I attended and didn't even need to try. I learnt to sit in meetings with a serene smile gazing into space; it was a form of business yoga.

One time I was asked by Terry to put in an appearance for the unveiling of a new name and identity for the Toyo Whalers, one of Japan's leading baseball teams. They were to become the Yokohama Baystars. Toyo is the world's largest fishing and fish-based company. It has huge fleets and enormous processing plants and is about the same overall size as Unilever. It owned the Whalers, but thought it was fair to rebrand them to reflect the city in which they were based, rather than the company that owned them – hence the change of name. I was invited to say a few words at the launch ceremony. It turned out to be an extraordinary trip.

I had no idea at all as to the passion with which Japanese fans support their baseball teams. A few days before the launch word had got out that Interbrand had conducted a rebranding exercise, including a new name, a redesign of the team's kit, a new mascot and a new logo, but before the official launch no one knew what the outcome was to be. Our offices in central Tokyo were besieged by fans for several days before the unveiling. The unveiling ceremony itself took place at a hotel in Yokohama, the port city adjacent to Tokyo. Seven hundred guests were invited, including virtually every major showbiz and sporting personality in the country, it would seem. It was carried live on Fuji TV, one of the key national channels, from 7pm until midnight. The stadium itself was packed to overflowing with many thousands of avid fans who followed the events on close circuit television. A special song had been recorded for the occasion by a leading pop star and it reached number one in the Japanese pop charts and stayed there for some weeks.

The President of Toyo made a speech, as did the manager of the club, Terry Oliver, me, a leading politician, a leading sports star and the captain of the team. Then the name and the new strip were revealed with great ceremony. The entire team walked out in their new uniforms, they were followed by dozens of models. There were fireworks and a huge fanfare. It was a sensation and everyone loved the result. But my main recollection of the evening was that suddenly the music and the lights dimmed and the spotlight fell on a huge, live king tuna, said to be four metres in length, which was wheeled in to the middle of the enormous hall. At a word of command, a dozen or so specially trained chefs sliced into the giant fish and the first pieces of raw sashimi were being consumed within sixty seconds. As an honoured guest, I was one of the first in the queue. It proved to be one of the most delicious dishes I had ever tasted, but I still feel guilty to have so enjoyed it – indeed, to have been part of that episode.

Terry and his team introduced branding to Japan and dominated the Japanese market. Indeed, Interbrand Japan still does. Soon a second office was opened in Osaka and then a Korean office in Seoul. Subsequently Terry oversaw the expansion of Interbrand's Asia-Pacific offices to include Singapore and Shanghai. Sadly, he died recently at his retirement home in Queensland. All his old friends met for dinner in London to remember his life and to raise a glass to an exceptional man and to his lovely wife Noriko.

The German and French offices, mentioned earlier, slowly developed in spite of their early problems, though, in my day, they were not the successes I would have wished. Nonetheless they provided an extremely valuable creative and research capability for the rest of the group. Other overseas offices were opened in Sydney, Australia, under the direction of David Andrew, and in Johannesburg, South Africa, the latter a joint venture business led by Jeremy Sampson, an expat South African who had returned to his home country after the fall of the apartheid regime. In Italy we opened an office in Milan run by Marco Gualdi. By the end of the 1980s we had a worldwide operation with a broadly based range of skills, three large, particularly profitable businesses and a number of smaller businesses each of which was growing and profitable. We thought we were pretty slick operators with a pretty slick business.

THE NIGHT OF THE LONG KNIVES

For some time we had been considering going public and in 1989 we spoke to our bankers and brokers and started to take this prospect seriously. Our financial performance that year was very good and the outlook was encouraging. We employed about 250 people worldwide and our pre-tax profits were close to 25% of turnover after paying all bonuses and profit shares. We were assured that the market would be very interested in a piece of the action, particularly as branding and brand valuation was, by this time, becoming a hot business topic. Among other things, we felt that a public quotation would help us grow faster as we would be able to make strategic acquisitions more readily.

But in early 1990 our world fell apart. New business in January 1990 was very soft everywhere, but particularly in the UK. We had allowed our overheads to creep up in the previous year, justifying this on the basis that we needed a more fulsome infrastructure for when we became a public company. The result was that in that first month of the year we made a thumping loss. I became very jittery, feeling in my bones that something was seriously wrong. My colleagues all disagreed. They told me that January was always a quiet month, that I was overreacting, that there was no cause for concern. Their assurances calmed me down a little.

February, however, was no better and my worries returned. Towards the end of that month I had an appointment in Amsterdam with Heineken, old and valued clients. On my return journey, while I was sitting on the plane at Schiphol airport, I noticed an old business acquaintance and competitor board the aircraft a moment before the doors closed. This person ran a huge London-based, publicly quoted design company; one that, a few years earlier, had been among those who had set up a naming company in competition with us. The late-arriving passenger took a seat in the row ahead of me. He spotted me as he was sitting down and said, "John, I need to talk to you. Can we travel back into London together?" I agreed.

When we arrived at Heathrow we set off together, but when we reached the sign for the Underground, my new companion kept going. I called to him that he was going the wrong way and he said that he wasn't, he had his chauffeur waiting for him. We sat in the back of his black chauffeur-driven BMW and started a serious business discussion. In effect, I found myself being offered his huge design company for nothing. I was aghast. I asked what on earth he was doing travelling around in a chauffeured car when his company was obviously in serious financial trouble. (I could sense his chauffeur listening intently to this conversation.) He ignored me on this point and we talked for a while about how Interbrand might take over his group. I think however that we both knew that his situation was hopeless.

First thing the next morning I called together all my directors and told them that I now knew with certainty that we were facing a crisis. We were not looking at a temporary blip in trading that was only affecting us. The situation was much more serious than this. We were seeing the start of a serious recession; when large companies find the going tough, the first thing they do is stop spending money with firms like ours. I related my discussion the previous evening and said that even though it was clear that one of the biggest design companies in Britain was in very serious trouble, I was damned if Interbrand was going the same way. However, if we continued to make the losses that we had made in January, we would be out of business by the summer, particularly as we had just moved to very expensive new offices in Covent Garden. My colleagues asked me what I was proposing and I said I required the UK overhead to be reduced forthwith by 40%. I also wanted Michael Birkin, my CEO, to speak to colleagues overseas and give them instructions to make all possible savings too. My briefing was not well received, but I think secretly they were all as worried as I was and knew I was right. After a heated discussion I got my way.

We cut deeply into the overhead (though not by 40% – we achieved a 20% reduction) and I was somewhat ashamed that there were so many costs that we could dispense with. For example, it transpired that one person in accounts spent most of her time sorting out problems with company cars. I insisted that all company cars were to go and so was she. We had also hired dedicated HR people, a function for which, until recently, we had not had any specialist staff. It also became apparent that a number of people were being retained because they were popular with colleagues and not because they were particularly competent or productive. All these went too.

All directors took a cut in salary and two floors of our offices were emptied to save on council tax. In due course, they were sub-let. Travel costs came under even closer scrutiny (I've always been a bitter opponent of expensive executive class travel, but people had proved highly skilled in circumventing my wishes on this) and every penny of expenditure was examined in detail. We had made huge losses in the first two months of 1990 and again in March, to which had to be added substantial redundancy costs. Our results for the first quarter of 1990 were, as a result, appalling. Fortunately we broke even in the second and third quarters and by the fourth quarter we were trading so successfully on a much-reduced cost base that we made back all the losses which had occurred earlier in the year. 1990 turned out to be a break-even year overall but our plans to go public had to be put on hold.

Later, whenever we discussed 'The Night of the Long Knives' we reflected how lucky we were to have detected the recession so promptly, thanks in large part to a chance meeting on a plane. We had our crisis early in the cycle, but in 1991, 1992 and 1993 we had one record year after another. Many design, marketing and advertising businesses ignored the early signs of recession and endured their hardest years later in the recession. Others did not make it.

13

POKER FACE

In which I learnt how to play 'poker' when selling a business and also what it was like to no longer be my own boss after twenty years.

After our serious 'speed wobble' early in 1990 we got the business back under control. Within a year or two our thoughts returned to the possibility of going public or even selling the business in its entirety. The new listings market was poor during the recession of the early 90s and not much was happening in the area of mergers and acquisitions, but we knew that when confidence returned, Interbrand would be a very interesting prospect.

The reasons why we considered a sale of some or all of the business were many, and no doubt each of us had particular issues which loomed large. I must admit that in my case greed played some part. I was comfortable financially but by no means wealthy. We paid ourselves fairly, but we did not take the huge salaries that seemed to be enjoyed by many of our contemporaries. I had a mortgage and the monthly credit card bills were not so insignificant in terms of my income as to go unnoticed. The prospect of no mortgage, money in the bank and spare funds to spend on antiques and a house in Italy was quite attractive. The same, I believe, was true of all the other directors, most of whom were much younger than me. For them, for example, the prospect of buying nice houses with in and out gravel drives was alluring.

But money played relatively a minor part. A more important factor for me was that I felt I had had my best years at Interbrand. I was coming up to fifty-years-old and found it difficult at times to generate the same enthusiasm as before when meeting a client or pitching for a new project. Many of the new projects seemed, too, to be familiar. I experienced often a sense of *dejá vu*, and even though I enjoyed winning new jobs, unless they were particularly novel or exciting I took much less pleasure in actually doing the work than I had before. I also found that clients were at times little over half my age. I began to feel like an older person marooned in a young person's world and this too was uncomfortable.

I also realised that I was essentially an entrepreneur, not a corporate man, but Interbrand needed to become more 'corporate' as it grew larger. I found this prospect curiously disquieting. I was not at all sure I would fit in. I also realised that unless I handed over even more management control to the other directors, they would become increasingly frustrated and might well leave. I had been used to knowing every single thing that went on in the business and to setting company standards in most areas. Increasingly I realised, however, that in sectors such as brand valuation, my colleagues were developing skills and methodologies that owed nothing to me and which at times I didn't even fully understand. I did not resent this, but realised that a baton change was taking place from the old guard, principally Tom Blackett and me, to the younger members of the team, and I needed to acknowledge this and act accordingly.

I reasoned that if we were to go public I could increasingly focus on 'chairman matters' – investor relations, writing, looking for acquisitions – and my colleagues could be given a more or less free rein to run the business. In this way we could grow the business, the value of our equity would rise steeply and everyone would be happy. And if we sold out entirely, all of us, me included, would be emancipated, all debts and obligations would have been paid off, and I could get on with the rest of my life.

DEALING WITH THE DEAL MAKERS

But there were some other particular issues that weighed with all of us. One of them was that we had a venture capital investor whom we had all come to dislike. The firm in question had spotted Interbrand almost ten years earlier and had approached us to say that they would like to take a small stake. We were flattered by their interest and felt it would be sensible to develop a relationship with such a company. At the time we were considering an expensive office move and knew that new money would help us kit out our new London headquarters to a high and impressive standard without borrowings. We therefore raised a small amount of venture capital through this company. None of us took any money personally. For the first few years we enjoyed a good relationship with the venture capitalists and the executives appointed to oversee their investment were bright and fun. Each side appeared happy with the relationship.

Things started to go wrong, however, when our investors wrote to me requesting that I circulate a note to all shareholders to say that if anyone wished to sell shares, they would be interested in buying them as they wished to increase their stake in the company. None of the executive team wished to sell shares but my sister, Eileen who had been with us at the start, but who had left to start a family, did. Her husband had been diagnosed with a serious illness and, with two young children, she needed to raise some cash. She agreed, reluctantly, to sell half her holding to this investment company. She was the only shareholder prepared to sell.

A couple of months later she phoned me in some distress. She said that the sale had been due to take place that very day, but the person handling the transaction for the venture capital company had just called her to say that though they still wanted to go ahead with the deal, they were reducing the price substantially – she could take or leave the lower price. She said that they must have somehow heard about her family situation and decided to take advantage of it. I was outraged as our company was trading more strongly all the time and there were no market reasons to renege on an agreed deal. It was a piece of unworthy opportunism. I phoned the person concerned and his attitude was clearly to chisel wherever possible. He showed no shame at his behaviour and refused to budge. I therefore phoned the chairman who was extremely embarrassed and agreed to go ahead with the original deal. He explained that his deal makers tended to get a little over-enthusiastic and greedy and he assured me this would never happen again.

Unfortunately it did happen again a year or two later and it transpired that it involved the same 'deal maker'. When we were planning the acquisition of the design company in Connecticut, which I have mentioned earlier, we looked at various ways of funding the deal, but knew that our existing investors would expect first refusal. They said they were, in fact, keen to be involved and put together a proposal whereby they would provide the $1 million initial payment, in return for more Interbrand shares. We accepted their proposal.

With this financing in place, Paul Stobart moved to New York to complete the acquisition and handle matters in the post-acquisition period. It was planned that the deal would be closed at the end of a working week, but, in the event, negotiations dragged on and the deal was not signed until the Sunday. The next day Paul phoned the investors in London to ask that the funds be released, as agreed. A few hours later he called me to say that no funds had arrived and he was coming under pressure from the other side's lawyers.

Frantic phone calls continued all the rest of the day between Paul in New York, Michael Birkin and me in London, the various advisers and the investors until eventually, late that afternoon, an assistant at that firm telephoned me. She was in tears and said that before she told me what was happening, she wanted to let me know that she had no part in the matter and, indeed, as a matter of principle had resigned over it.

She went on to say that she had responsibility for transferring the funds and had been just about to do so that morning, when her boss told her that she must inform us that she could only do so if we agreed a substantial arrangement fee. She said that she knew that this had never been agreed and it was totally improper, but it was the way her boss did business and she'd had enough of it. She said if I didn't agree to it, she couldn't release any funds and we would obviously have serious problems, having already made the acquisition. I reluctantly agreed to the arrangement fee – I had no choice – but I was determined to reverse it.

The next morning I phoned the chairman's office once again, but he wasn't there. I tried several more times during that day and eventually his secretary told me that all the directors of the firm were attending a private three-day conference away from the office at a luxury hotel and spa to determine long-term corporate strategy. She mentioned the name of the hotel, saying that the chairman would be there all the next day, but had left strict instructions that he could not be contacted under any circumstances.

The next morning I set off early and drove to the Chewton Glen Hotel in the New Forest, about one hundred miles south-west of London. When the directors broke mid-morning for coffee, I was waiting outside the conference room and demanded a private word with the chairman. He was taken aback, but had no choice but to hear me out as he obviously had an extremely angry and determined client on his hands. I told him the story and, for a second time, he reversed the dirty dealing of his subordinate. He said the problem was that this person was the firm's best fee-earner and he was reluctant to discipline or fire him.

I said that I thought this was utter madness as well as immoral. The result of his behaviour over the purchase of my sister's shares was that I had already dissuaded at least half a dozen companies from going to his firm for venture capital and I would continue now to issue negative reports. How many other John Murphys were out there destroying the reputation of his company as a result of the activities of this one man? He said he recognised the problem and perhaps it was time to act. I don't know if he did so or not.

CAPPING A PROBLEM

These two incidents left a very nasty taste in our mouths, but they were not the sum total of our dissatisfaction with these investors. At the time of the original deal, we had agreed a cap on directors' salaries so that the directors could not distribute all the profits of the business to themselves by way of salary and bonus, thus defrauding the external shareholders who otherwise would share *pro-rata* in any profits and dividends. When we agreed the overall cap we enquired, as part of the negotiations, what would happen to the cap when the company grew and acquired more directors? Also, what would happen when the salary cap became too small due to inflation and the passage of time? We were assured that we could sit down with them periodically and agree an increased cap – they promised us they would not be difficult and that such a cap was standard practice. The purpose of the cap, they assured us, was simply to protect their interests and we would have no problems at all with agreeing a new cap as the company grew.

Over the coming years we did add more directors and the growth of the business, coupled with the relatively high rates of inflation in the 1980s, meant that our total directors' salary bill started to bump up against the cap. The implications of this were that any salary payments in excess of the cap were deemed to be a distribution and the investors became due an extra dividend based upon this so called 'distribution'. Thus the investors, who by this time owned 30% of the business, would, if the cap were £500,000 and the salaries totalled £750,000, receive a payment of 30% of £250,000 in addition to the 30% of true profits which they were already entitled to.

Accordingly, when we started to approach the agreed cap we asked their representative on our board to address this problem and we were assured this would be sorted out promptly. But for month after month and year after year nothing was, in fact, done despite our repeated requests. Our investors received higher and higher dividends and utterly refused to do anything about increasing the cap. We were fobbed off with excuses and promises, but it was clear that the promises they had made at the time they first invested were worth nothing.

By the early 1990s, a disproportionate share of our profits was going into the hands of the venture capitalists. Eventually, they admitted to me that they had no intention of altering the arrangement, as it was so profitable and times were hard; none of their other investments were doing as well as us, so they intended to milk us. If we really wanted to get shot of them, they said, we must either go public or we must sell out entirely so that their special rights fell away. I started to realise that I had been foolish to believe what we had been told, although I also knew that such behaviour was by no means that of all venture capitalists.

MURPHY OF MURPHY'S LAW

One other apparently insignificant incident also steered me in the direction of a sale or flotation. When brand valuation first burst on the scene in the late 1980s, Interbrand became a hot name on the conference circuit. We were inundated with requests for speakers and as chairman I bore the brunt. By the early 1990s the team from the London office was giving around one hundred public lectures a year at conferences, business schools and so forth, and I handled close to half of these, my co-directors the rest. I spoke all over the world on branding, brand valuation, the future of brands and how to develop great brands and grew to hate it. As soon as I had finished one talk, I would have to start planning the next. Every one filled me with dread; I envied speakers who could stand up in public without gnawing fear, as I couldn't.

There then occurred an incident that still brings me out in cold sweats. I gave a talk on branding to a major conference in Amsterdam, which, I was assured, had been well received and which had led to a great deal of comment in the Dutch press. A couple of weeks later I received a call from the office of the Dean at the Post-Graduate Technical University in Eindhoven, Holland, who asked me if I would be prepared to come to the university to give the same talk to the post-graduates and the teaching faculty as I had given in Amsterdam. I said I'd be happy to do so and we fixed a date.

On the day in question I flew to Eindhoven from London's City Airport and was met by the Dean. When we reached the university, I noticed scores of posters on the walls announcing my talk; my name was also prominently displayed on TV monitors. I was obviously being given quite a build up. We then walked in to the main lecture theatre. I stood at the front, chatting to the Dean as he waited to introduce me. Looking around, I noticed that the huge lecture theatre was jam-packed. All the seats were taken and people were sitting on every step. Extra seating had also been provided at the front, sides and back of the auditorium. There was a serious buzz of excitement.

I turned to the Dean just before he introduced me and whispered: "What a fantastic turnout. There must be 500 people here. Why have so many people come to hear me talk about branding?" He turned to me, looking confused and said, "Branding? What's branding?" I said it was what I had come to talk about. He replied, "No, you've come to talk about Murphy's Law. You are the Murphy of Murphy's Law, aren't you?" With a sinking heart I replied, "No, I'm the Murphy of branding, not the Murphy of Murphy's Law. I know nothing about Murphy's Law." He then told me he had made a terrible mistake and had billed me as the Murphy of Murphy's Law. The audience had come to hear about this famous law, not about branding.

If I had been able to do so, I would have fled instantly. As it was, I received a thirty-second introduction from the Dean and dived straight in. I started my talk by saying that we all know about Murphy's Law, which states that everything that can go wrong, will go wrong. Unfortunately, I was now able to provide them with a perfect example of the application of this law. I said that there had been some sort of mix-up and I was standing there to talk to them about branding; I was not the inventor or discoverer of Murphy's Law. I then addressed them on the subject of branding for the next forty-five minutes. At the end of my talk, I received polite applause and was presented with a bottle of Geneva gin and an illustrated book on tulips. I was then taken back to the airport where I downed several strong beers at the bar before getting on the plane. I was still trembling when I got off the plane in London – and not from the effect of the beers.

I later discovered that a major Dutch business newspaper had reported my earlier talk in Amsterdam under the heading 'Murphy's Law'. The article went on to say that the particular business law expounded by John Murphy of Interbrand was to do with the importance of brands. However, someone at the university had simply read the headline and the name Interbrand, not the text, and had jumped to the conclusion that I was the better known

Murphy. My dislike of public speaking became even stronger after this incident. Indeed, as I have said, thinking about this incident still makes me feel mildly nauseous. However, public speaking was so much a part of my role that I knew the best escape route for me from any further public speaking was probably to sell the business and push off. I was, accordingly, increasingly drawn towards an outright sale rather than a flotation where I would have to remain as chairman and company spokesman.

GOING PUBLIC

We decided, however, to proceed in parallel with the planning of both a sale and a flotation. We knew that the tom-toms were announcing that we were possibly up for sale, so no active initiatives were needed at that point in order to lure a purchaser; we mainly focused our minds and efforts on a flotation. From early 1992 onwards, we made serious plans for a public offering. We interviewed merchant banks and brokers and appointed legal advisers. We also did whatever tidying up they considered necessary of our financial and other systems even though we were already operating, in large part, to the standards of a public company so did not have too much to do. Nor did we have too many skeletons in our closet. Our trading 'blip' in early 1990 took, of course, a bit of explaining and I also had to explain the failure of Buffalo Discount Warehouses in the early 80s and my role in this, but neither of these matters was felt to be a serious impediment to a public flotation.

Overall, it was felt that Interbrand would arouse a great deal of market interest. Based in large part on our brand valuation activities, we were very well known to investors and were rightly regarded as being at the forefront of the marketing world. We also had an extensive blue chip client list, lots of repeat business and a truly international presence. Furthermore, our margins were strong, we had exceptional growth and we had an impressive team of people. There seemed no doubt that any offering would be very well received, though the market was still relatively quiet and we would need to wait for the right moment to come along.

But a public flotation also had its down side, particularly for me. It seemed that investors would not be happy at my cashing in too many of my chips at the time of the flotation and they would also expect me to stay on in the company for the foreseeable future. The opportunity to sell more shares over the coming years would also be limited as there was a danger that whenever I sold a few shares, it could be interpreted by the market as a lack of confidence in the business. In other words, I could realise some money at the outset but after that I could do little to raise funds for myself.

Given that I was coming up to my fiftieth birthday and had always had in mind that by the time I was fifty I would have made my pile, and would devote myself to a life of mucking about, I was not too happy at the prospect of being locked in for years to come. Similar problems existed for all my colleagues. There was also another factor – that I would have to be seen as remaining in the driving seat, at least as far as the City was concerned, so one specific objective, that of giving some really competent people their heads, might not be fully met. As I pondered the options, I came to be even more convinced that a sale of the entire business might be preferable to a public offering of part of it.

We debated the pros and cons for months and finally decided to pay more attention than we had done to an outright trade sale. Over the years we had been approached by dozens of potential acquirers, but the really strong prospects seemed to us to be the major advertising agency groups such as WPP, Interpublic or Omnicom. After all, these were the people with the money. Moreover, most of the smaller players seemed to be looking for a merger rather than an outright cash purchase, but were any deal to be other than an outright cash purchase, we would sooner go on the market, we decided. We approached each of the three major advertising groups and one, Omnicom, responded extremely positively.

TALKING WITH OMNICOM

Omnicom is a huge business. At that time – mid 1993 – it employed over 20,000 people and had three worldwide advertising networks: DDB, BBDO and TBWA. It also had a fourth arm known as Diversified Agency Services (DAS), a loose grouping of companies that included PR agencies, design groups, merchandising companies and other specialist marketing-related businesses. Indeed, DAS was, and probably still is, Omnicom's largest division, overall.

Though all of us had doubts about selling out to an ad agency, the senior managers of Omnicom were clearly competent. They saw themselves as managers of a business that happened to have large holdings in advertising and not as advertising professionals with the neuroses and conceits of that business.

We got to know John Wren, President of DAS (and soon to be CEO of Omnicom), and Peter Jones, President of DAS Europe, well. They seemed to understand Interbrand and appeared extremely impressed with our business and our people. They convinced us that Interbrand would flourish as part of the Omnicom group. They also felt that the valuation methodologies we had developed could be extremely valuable to the advertising agencies, even though the agencies themselves had not yet woken up to this.

Overall we all felt it would be a good match. Our senior people would have exceptional prospects, Omnicom had the deep pockets needed for further acquisitions, and we were assured that Omnicom would be there to help as required but would not interfere. They also appeared ready to pay a fair price. But all this turned out to be only partly true.

THE OFFER

A team from Omnicom's New York office carried out a major due diligence exercise on Interbrand and, in autumn 1993, offered £12.5m for the business (in current values this price needs to be multiplied several times) plus the prospect of a modest top-up based upon a one year earn-out. I found that the prospect of receiving several million pounds was enticing. However there was a problem: our advisers were quite certain that we would float at a valuation of £15million or more. It seemed crazy, on careful reflection, to sell the business to Omnicom for substantially less than the valuation that the market would put on the business.

I thought about Omnicom's offer for some time and our deliberations reached a crisis at a board meeting in London. The negotiations with Omnicom had been handled mainly by Michael Birkin, Group MD, Chuck Brymer, President of Interbrand US and Noel Penrose, Group Finance Director. They clearly favoured the Omnicom offer and were keen that we accept it. It was, after all, a cash offer and relatively uncomplicated. I also knew that Omnicom had probably hinted to each of them about their glittering prospects in the event of an Omnicom takeover of Interbrand. Each of these colleagues tried to be as balanced, fair, and objective as possible but there was little doubt as to where their enthusiasms lay.

The rest of the board was less convinced, the major stumbling block being the offer price. Eventually it came down to me to make a decision. I said that it was pretty clear that once Omnicom took over I would become a figurehead at best, so for me a very important factor was that of price, not my career prospects, and I was not prepared to accept an offer below the flotation value. I said that I would call Omnicom the next day and tell them that their offer was simply not good enough and we would go on the market instead.

At this point Noel Penrose spoke up saying that this would probably not be possible. I asked him why and he told me that if I did not accept the Omnicom offer, he would resign and if he resigned we would be unable to float, as no company could float without a finance director or if it had had a recent change of finance director. I stopped the meeting and asked Noel if we could have a private word outside.

We went into the corridor and I asked him to repeat what he had said to me in the board meeting. He said it was quite simple. If I rejected the Omnicom offer, he would resign forthwith and therefore we could not float. So I had a choice, accept Omnicom's offer or get nothing, at least for some years. I told him that I still planned to reject the Omnicom offer so by definition, he had handed me his resignation, which I accepted. I would like him to pack up his things immediately and leave the building within the hour, which he did. I returned to the meeting and told my colleagues what had happened and we got on with the planning of our flotation.

Curiously, when I spoke to our brokers the next morning, they were not at all concerned at the turn of events. They said they thought Noel was a good financial director, as we all did, but they said that people do strange things and the market would not be too upset by the departure of our financial director – they could handle it. They also told me that they knew of someone who was available immediately and would be a great replacement for Noel. The person in question, Sue Couldery, joined us a few days later and proved to be a first class finance director.

GOING THE EXTRA MILE

But even though I had rejected the Omnicom offer, I would still have preferred a trade sale to a flotation. But I also suspected that all was not lost, as I was reasonably confident that Omnicom would come back with a higher offer before too long.

And so it proved; a few weeks later Omnicom increased its offer substantially. I was inclined to accept the new offer and knew that the external investors, as well as most directors, were all in favour of the bid. Thus once I accepted the new offer it would, in effect, be a done deal. (At that point, outside investors held almost one third of the shares, the directors about 20% and my wife and I the rest; however, my wife and I distributed more shares to directors and staff immediately before the deal so that, at the time of signature, each party – the outside investors, the Interbrand directors and staff, and my wife and I – held about one third each.) However, I decided to sleep on the offer for a few days – it was not going to go away – though I did not share my likely acceptance of the deal with my colleagues in case I had second thoughts. But a few days later I accepted the increased offer.

A MEDICAL CASE STUDY

The deal itself proved to be relatively painless. The only major problem we had was with the venture capital company, our major outside investor. They thought that the deal we had done with Omnicom was fantastic and that it benefited shareholders greatly, but they proved to be a nightmare during the detailed drafting and negotiations.

The senior executive they nominated to handle matters on their behalf was so anxious and indecisive that he drove everyone else mad. Indeed, the partner of the law firm acting for them during the sale negotiations became so angry at the antics of his client that he finally snapped. He suddenly stood up and shouted at his client that he was a complete idiot and incompetent and he never wanted to have anything to do with him or his company again. He then stormed out of the meeting. His firm had to hurriedly find someone else to replace him. He almost lost them a major client. Nevertheless, the deal finally got done. But the outside investors had one further unpleasant surprise for me. Perhaps, in light of their earlier behaviour, I shouldn't have been surprised.

Once we had accepted Omnicom's offer, but before we started detailed negotiations and drafting, I had suggested to all shareholders that we be represented by one lawyer who would act for all shareholders. I further proposed that we settled this lawyer's bill *pro rata*. Everyone agreed to this, though the venture capitalists said that they might also appoint a second lawyer to look after their particular interests, which they did. However, they would, they said, be happy to pay their share of the cost of the main lawyer acting for all the vendors, as he would much reduce the work their own lawyer would have to do.

When the deal was finalised and I had received the final account from our excellent lawyer, David James, payable by all the vendors, I settled it and then asked all the parties for their share. At this point the venture capitalists said that they had changed their minds and they weren't prepared to pay their share after all! I protested, but was so weary of them by this stage I decided to pay their share out of my own pocket, as I clearly could not ask the other shareholders to cough up more. Besides, I had a pretty deep pocket at that time. But I was still very angry.

The takeover by Omnicom worked pretty well for Interbrand and its staff. Chuck Brymer became Group Chief Executive of Interbrand and is now President of DDB, one of Omnicom's huge advertising agency chains. Michael Birkin moved to New York to run DAS and later was put in charge of Omnicom's Asian activities having also been appointed vice chairman of Omnicom. (He is not, however, with Omnicom any longer, having moved to Hakuhodo, a major Japanese agency to handle their non-Japanese acquisitions programme.) Paul Stobart left Interbrand and joined Sage, becoming chairman, Europe; he now runs a major medical electronics company. Tom Blackett remained with Interbrand until retirement. Now Interbrand is a company with, I am told, well over 1000 employees and a turnover of $200m, though some of this comes from acquisitions rather than organic growth.

MOVING ON

But what about me? The acquisition provided me with a substantial amount of cash, but on a personal level it was less satisfactory. Omnicom was less 'hands off' than I'd been led to believe. And after being my own boss for twenty years, I was frustrated that some extravagant promises made to secure the sale were not fulfilled.

I continued as chairman of Interbrand, nominally at least, for a little over two years after the sale. The arrangement I had made with John Wren was that I would run the group and would have total discretion in doing so, short, of course, of buying an executive jet or doing something equally daft. Omnicom, with all its resources, would, however, be there to help wherever they could. It sounded great and I largely bought into the plan, though I was not so unworldly as to believe that business life as part of Omnicom would be exactly as it had been before. In fact, it was very different.

I am not especially bitter about my 'Omnicom experience' and nor am I particularly surprised. I knew that anyone buying Interbrand would find it an utterly fascinating company, full of talent and innovation, and so it proved. It was simply too juicy a company for its new owner to stand aside from it. Interbrand was such a wonderful business that Omnicom wanted to 'own' its success and my continuing presence was a hindrance to this. I was 'old Interbrand'; the Interbrand of Omnicom was the future.

Anyway, I had my own plans: I had decided to put some of my branding theory into practice by becoming a brand owner.

14

THE SPIRIT OF BRANDING

In which I stumbled across an opportunity to build a great luxury drinks brand, Plymouth Gin, and decided to put my branding experience into practice, thus moving from brand consultant to brand owner.

I don't know whether other business consultants suffer similar self doubts, but I always had a niggling worry at the back of my mind that the advice on branding I had been giving to my clients for so many years might be pure tosh. I therefore decided that I would use part of the proceeds from the sale of Interbrand to become a brand owner in order to put some of the branding theory, which I had been spouting for so long, into practice. I believed profoundly in the value and power of brands and was convinced that if I developed a brand or brands of my own, I could make a great deal of money and enjoy myself along the way. But how to transform the wish into reality?

A MEETING OF KINDRED SPIRITS

As soon as I sold Interbrand I started, with Omnicom's agreement, to develop my plans to become a brand owner. My first scheme was to start a brewery and I will tell you more about this in Chapter 16. But while I was developing this plan, a second opportunity came my way.

One Monday morning, while sitting at my desk at Interbrand, I received a call from my bank manager. He told me that he was not calling on banking business, but on a personal matter. He had had a drink over that weekend with an old school friend of his who had worked in the spirits industry for many years, and who had a project for which he was trying to find backers.

Given my interest in beer, might I also be interested in spirits? I said I would be pleased to meet his friend and a couple of hours later, this man and two of his business partners turned up at my office.

They told me that all three of them had been directors of James Burroughs, the distillers of Beefeater Gin, though when it had become part of Whitbread they had all left and set up their own consultancy businesses. Later Whitbread had sold Beefeater Gin to Allied Domecq and that in turn had led to a business opportunity that they hoped might interest me.

It transpired that Allied Domecq wanted to sell Plymouth Gin as there wasn't room in their portfolio for two premium gin brands – Beefeater and Plymouth. It seemed that they had even considered closing down Plymouth Gin, but in view of its long history and its place in the affections of the people of Plymouth, they were worried about the negative publicity a closure would generate. They had, therefore, decided to put Plymouth Gin on the market.

The three ex-directors of Beefeater believed that Plymouth Gin could be bought for less than £1 million. They were able to put together between them perhaps 10% of the likely purchase price and were seeking individuals who would put up the balance. In return for spotting the opportunity and managing the new business for the new investors, they would expect a further 10% of the business as options. They said they had a Dutch investor, Fred van Woerkom, who was prepared to put up 45% of the purchase price in return for 40% of the equity. Would I match him?

From the outset I was interested. For a start, the role of the brand in the success of a premium spirits operation is huge and almost matches that of fragrances or luxury accessories. It was, accordingly, an opportunity that I would relish.

DISTILLING THE OFFER

But there was another attraction for me. A few years earlier, when I had been putting together the Interbrand book *The World's Greatest Brands* I included a section on the world's great spirits brands – Absolut Vodka, Smirnoff, Johnnie Walker and the rest. I also included Beefeater Gin, but was surprised, when I came to write about this brand and its sector, how comparatively boring Beefeater appeared to be and how lacking the gin sector was in innovation or vitality. By contrast, the vodka sector was booming and new vodka brands and variants were being introduced almost by the week. The market was awash with Polish vodkas, Russian vodkas, Icelandic vodkas, flavoured vodkas, coloured vodkas and all sorts of vodka-based premixed drinks. The investment and innovation in the vodka sector had led to huge growth and, as a result, vodka had long since overtaken gin, the preferred white spirit of previous generations.

So while all this was going on in vodka, the gin sector had languished. There were very few premium gin brands on the market – in effect only Gordon's, Beefeater, Bombay and Tanqueray – and the investment in these had been relatively modest, with almost no innovation or exciting marketing activity. As a result the gin market was in decline, though it was still large. I can remember wondering at the time why the world's great spirits companies invested such huge sums of money in, usually, relatively tasteless and boring vodkas when, it seemed to me, more modest investments in gin brands might yield much higher returns. Accordingly, when an opportunity came along to invest in Plymouth Gin, I found the prospect attractive.

Another thing which appealed to me was that, if Plymouth Gin proved successful, the business could most likely be easily sold – it would surely find a ready market, as most of the world's major spirits businesses did not own a premium gin: Allied Domecq owned Beefeater, Bacardi owned Bombay and Diageo owned both Gordon's and Tanqueray but the likes of Pernod Ricard, Brown Forman, Seagram and Suntory had nothing in the premium gin sector. These were all big, rich companies and surely would pay a high price for an emerging premium gin brand?

There were, however, problems with Plymouth Gin, or so I was told. For a start, even though it had been a successful and much respected brand for most of the 19th century and through into the mid 20th century, it was now, in effect, dead. Annual sales were only about two or three thousand cases. However, it seemed possible that fans of the brand might return to it if it became more widely available for them to buy.

I was also told that even though any sale would include the historic distillery on Plymouth's Barbican together with a skilled head distiller and a small supporting team, nothing else would be included in the sale apart from a sheaf of trade mark certificates. All other business services – financial services, company secretarial, marketing, sales, distribution, public relations, human resources and so forth – had been provided centrally by Allied Domecq and would cease with the sale. We would therefore need to finance substantial losses for many months from the date of purchase and would also need to invest heavily in the development of the business infrastructure and especially in the critically important areas of sales, marketing and distribution.

On the plus side, the three people who brought the business opportunity to me assured me that they knew the gin market backwards and could turn the business around very, very quickly. They would manage the business magnificently and any losses would only be short term.

That Monday morning I listened to their proposal with interest, and agreed to travel to Plymouth on the Wednesday to meet the team and view the distillery. When I arrived there, the head distiller and the rest of the staff greeted me warmly, and it quickly became apparent that they were competent, honest and likeable. I was also impressed with the distillery itself, though it had become somewhat run-down and required, at the very least, some tender loving care.

A STORY OF THE SEA

The Plymouth Gin brand itself was, however, the major revelation. I had heard of Plymouth Gin but had no idea how much history and 'texture' the brand possessed. I walked around the distillery in a daze, listening to the fascinating story of Plymouth Gin. The company dated from 1793 when a distillery had been set up in Plymouth to supply the needs of the Royal Navy. At that time, all Royal Navy officers received a substantial daily allowance of high proof gin. Naval ratings received a similar allowance of rum. Both officers and men were expected to dilute these spirits prior to their consumption. The practice of serving alcohol to both officers and men dated from 1740 and continued until 1970, and was prompted initially by the poor quality of drinking water available on board His Majesty's ships.

In the late 18th century, each of the major Royal Navy bases (for example, Plymouth, Portsmouth and Chatham) had its own distillery to supply Britain's fighting fleets, but Plymouth Gin quickly became the preferred gin on account of its smoothness and the fact that it could be readily mixed with water, a unique property among gins. During the 19th century, when Britannia ruled the waves, the Royal Navy took Plymouth Gin to the four corners of the earth and by the end of the century, it was one of the world's earliest power brands.

In the 1920s and 1930s, Plymouth Gin benefited from the popularity of cocktails and other mixed drinks. Indeed, the first-ever recorded dry martini recipe specified that it should only be made with Plymouth Gin. Between the wars, North America became far and away the most important market for the brand, in spite of Prohibition. It is reported that Plymouth Gin was a favourite of both Roosevelt and Churchill. It was served on Nile pleasure cruisers, in the White House, on the Santa Fe railroad and on the Titanic. At home, retired naval officers drank Plymouth Gin, just as they had learned to do in the navy, as a pink gin, that is with water and a dash of Angostura bitters (both water and Angostura bitters were provided in ward rooms without charge whereas mixer drinks had to be paid for). Plymouth Gin also brought considerable recognition and prosperity to the city of Plymouth.

HARD TIMES

However, from the 1950s onwards, Plymouth Gin fell on hard times and the ending of the Naval gin ration in 1970 didn't help this. In the immediate post-war period it had suffered from raw materials rationing and the business later passed through various hands, losing a bit of momentum each time. By the time it became part of Allied Domecq, sales were in serious decline and the main customer base appeared to consist of a declining band of retired Royal Navy officers and a few elderly enthusiasts in the United States, Japan, Australia and the UK. By the early 1990s only two or three thousand cases of this wonderful gin were being sold worldwide each year.

My visit to Plymouth that Wednesday in early 1996 filled me with excitement, but I also realised that any rescuer of the business would face a daunting task. The history of the brand and the quality of the product were strong positives and the fact that a large freehold distillery was included in the purchase provided a strong underpinning. Nonetheless, it was clear that the brand had no momentum whatsoever and getting it back on its feet would be a major undertaking.

I was, however, determined to give it a go. The next day I confirmed my interest in putting up 45% of the probable purchase price of around £1 million and I called the other interested investor, Fred van Woerkom in Rotterdam, to confirm that I was on board. Later that day we submitted an offer to Allied Domecq, and the very next day they accepted our offer. At the beginning of the week I had barely heard of Plymouth Gin; by the end of the week it was, in effect, partly mine.

Sorting out the paperwork took the lawyers only a few weeks, but along the way my accountants advised me that such a large stakeholding would create serious tax problems for me. They advised that there should be three major investors, not two, and that each investor should have a shade under 30% of the business.

A BUSINESS OF THREE

They introduced to us a potential third investor, Richard Koch, a well known business guru, consultant and investor, who had built up his own strategic consultancy practice and been instrumental in the development of Filofax. I talked him through the Plymouth Gin story and he shared my enthusiasm. I also went to Rotterdam to meet Fred van Woerkom and concluded that he would make an excellent business partner. There was one small issue, however – Fred lived in Rotterdam and Richard spent most of his time in Cape Town. They were both happy to be investors but required me to be chairman in order to safeguard their interests. Fortunately, this suited me well as the prospect of turning round Plymouth Gin excited me greatly.

HOME FROM HOME

Over the next few weeks I spent a great deal of time with the three gin experts who had introduced the business to us and who, we had agreed, would run the business on a day-to-day basis. However, it transpired that they had not worked for James Burroughs for a decade or more and none of them truly had much experience in general management or in marketing.

Within weeks it became apparent that turning around the business was not likely to be a job they could successfully accomplish. Their plan had been to work together as a sort of 'management co-operative'. Each would work separately from home, and each would maintain his existing business interests. I realised that this laid-back, hands-off management style would not be enough to ensure the business succeeded.

As a result, my relationship with them deteriorated sharply over the weeks and I became seriously worried, not just for my own sake, but also because I felt responsible for the investments made by Fred and Richard. Matters soon reached a head; I called them in for a lunchtime meeting to discuss matters and warned them that our discussion would be open and frank. This was only some six weeks or so after we had completed on the purchase.

AN INTERROGATION

I booked a table at St John, the fine restaurant on St John Street, near Smithfield in Central London. This was a favourite haunt of mine and just around the corner from my new London office. It became apparent over lunch that they felt that the business was theirs, not mine and that of the other investors. They resented my making any enquiries at all as to what progress was being made. I, for my part, was determined to find out what was going on. I needed progress urgently with reviving the business as we were losing money at the rate of £30,000 a month and the working capital we had provided was disappearing fast.

Over lunch I asked what had been done to implement the business plan they had presented to me and the other investors prior to the purchase. I was told, 'Things are going well', 'We're getting quite a lot of interest', 'We've had a lot of support from the trade', and so forth, but no specifics.

I decided I'd better be more incisive. I had been told that scores of major US importers would be interested in taking on the Plymouth Gin brand in that hugely important market; I asked for specific information on this. Again I was told nothing – 'Things are coming along nicely', 'We should have somebody on board soon'. Whenever I asked for specifics, I was fobbed off. Indeed, one of the three said to me, in exasperation, "Why do you need to know this. What's it to you?"

I patiently explained that I represented all three major investors and we had put up a great deal of money based upon the business plan they had prepared and assurances they had given. We owned at the time 90% of the business and, of course, were passionately interested in the progress of our investment. Moreover, I was an experienced businessman with particular skills in branding and was committed to use these skills to help develop Plymouth Gin. Did this explain why I was asking questions?

I soon realised that nothing had been done about the US market and that their claims to 'know the US market well' could probably not be substantiated; therefore, I turned my questioning closer to home. Prior to the purchase, I and the other investors had been told that Tesco would be interested in stocking Plymouth Gin and that speaking to Tesco would be one of their first priorities. I therefore asked what had been done in the previous weeks to interest Tesco? When was Tesco approached? What was Tesco's response?

Again I was fobbed off and here too, virtually nothing appeared to have been done. I found myself in the role of incredulous interrogator while they became increasingly angry interrogatees. Finally one of them said, "John, I really resent you asking me these questions about our company." I was, as they say, gob-smacked.

However, I had no wish to run Plymouth Gin myself, but nor was I prepared to let it drift. My sole interest was in the success of the company and if we could achieve this, all of us would do well. I asked them, accordingly, whether they were with me or not? I was assured that they were with me, and after lunch we returned to the office for some detailed planning.

Unfortunately, it never could or would work out, or so I came to believe. It became all too obvious that the gulf between the requirements of the investors and the performance that the so-called professional managers could deliver was unbridgeable. Soon, we parted company. Later, the three of us bought back the shares of the departing directors.

THE HOT SEAT

Now I was in a fix. I wanted to be an investor in, and non-executive chairman of, Plymouth Gin. I did not want to run it. But unexpectedly, I now found myself in the hot seat. We had a distillery in Plymouth capable of producing at least 200,000 cases of gin a year, sales of only 3000 cases, substantial ongoing losses, a rapidly declining cash balance, production expertise, but no sales expertise and investors in Holland and South Africa who were expecting me to protect their investments. I needed a chief executive, but meanwhile I had to take charge and get things moving.

In an attempt to recruit a new CEO, I first went through my personal list of contacts, but drew a blank. I knew some very competent people at

Interbrand, but felt that I was not in a position to poach staff from that source. I also knew lots of people in branded goods businesses, but most of them were quite senior and I did not relish the idea of luring someone away from a good job to the uncertainties of Plymouth Gin unless they had already indicated a wish to move on, and I could think of no one in this category.

After months of ineffectual searching, I decided to advertise in the trade and the national press. I offered a good salary plus stock options and had a strong response, but, after interviewing a number of candidates, did not feel that I had found the right person. Finally Richard Koch said that he had heard of an individual who was looking for a challenge and might fit the bill. His name was Charles Rolls and we appointed him managing director almost a year or so after we had bought the business.

Fortunately, prior to Charles's arrival, I had been able to familiarise myself with the business and identify policies we should follow and these served us well over the coming years.

By the time Charles joined us, all three investors had agreed on the broad direction we should be taking the business. We had also appointed a UK distributor who was starting to build sales in our important home market, and I had briefed Interbrand's design department to carry out a redesign of the bottle and of the label and get-up – Interbrand did not, at that time, have a strong packaging design portfolio, especially in spirits, so they offered me a special rate for the design assignment provided they could use the work for promotional purposes. I readily agreed. So by the time Charles Rolls joined, many of the diagnostics had been completed and certain key initiatives, such as the package redesign, were already in hand. Charles was, accordingly, able to hit the ground running.

Charles is a charismatic, energetic and highly competent man. He had trained as a mining engineer at Imperial College and then worked in the deep gold mines of South Africa. When he returned to the UK he joined a scientific and technical consultancy practice, but did not take to the world of consulting and was anxious to work for himself. He had tried one or two things, but nothing had worked out and at the time he was introduced to me through Richard Koch, he was 'between jobs'.

Even though Charles had no close knowledge or experience of the spirits industry or of branded goods in general, he took to Plymouth Gin very readily. Unlike many people, he had an instinctive understanding of brands and grasped immediately what branding was all about. He also loved the product and the production process and was very much at home in Plymouth and the West Country. Charles quickly made an impact and we worked together as a good team, with me focusing mainly on strategy and branding and him on running the business on a day-to-day basis.

Charles also understood the need for urgency, realising that our financial resources were necessarily limited and were being eroded fast. He had not hitherto had experience of public relations, but fully supported the notion that our only feasible means of driving forward sales was to put serious effort into PR, focusing on the quality and history of the brand. Charles loved dealing with journalists and his charm and passion for the brand quickly led to extensive supportive reviews in British journals and newspapers.

OUR BBC 2 MOMENT

However, the most important piece of PR that we ever received was entirely fortuitous and was not down to our efforts or those of our PR advisors. One day we received a phone call from a TV executive and were told, somewhat mysteriously, to watch the Food and Drink programme on BBC2 that evening. When we did so, we found that a large section of that night's programme was devoted to gin, a highly unusual piece of programming given that gin was not at all a fashionable drink at that time, in fact, the reverse.

The programme's drinks expert, Jilly Goolden (henceforth known within Plymouth Gin as St Jilly), started her piece by holding up a bottle of Gordon's gin. She said that Gordon's gin was Britain's favourite gin and accounted for about half of the British market, but she advised viewers to look carefully at the front label. She said that if you looked closely, you would notice that the alcoholic strength of Gordon's gin was no longer 40%, but had been quietly dropped to 37.5%, the weakest strength you can use for gin and still refer to it as gin. She said that this drop in strength saved the producer millions of pounds a year in excise duty, but did nothing for the taste of the product. She said that gin ought to be drunk at a minimum strength of 40% alcohol by volume.

Having launched this attack on the market leader, she then announced that she and the team had carried out a careful tasting of all the gins on the UK market, some thirty in all, including supermarkets' private label products. She followed by announcing, dramatically, that the best gin they had tasted was Plymouth Gin. She went on to eulogise the brand at some length, praising it for its subtlety, softness on the palate and mixability.

At that time the Food and Drink programme had about five million viewers (out of a total UK population approaching sixty million) and was hugely influential. Moreover, the viewers tended to be older and more affluent – just the people we were trying to reach with the Plymouth Gin story. First thing the next morning our phones started ringing.

GIN, GLORIOUS GIN

Over the course of the previous year we had managed to increase our UK sales, from around 2,500 cases per annum to 9,000, but we were finding the going tough. The major supermarket chains such as ASDA and Tesco were prepared to stock our brand in the West Country (due to its Plymouth origins) or on a special promotional basis, but were not interested in the permanent national listings which we needed.

The TV programme changed all that. Within days we had secured national listings with all the major supermarkets and off licence chains. Our new and much improved package design was introduced, by coincidence, virtually the same week. We had also appointed Remy Cointreau as our UK distributors to coincide with the introduction of the new pack design.

Almost overnight we went from being a minor national brand to being a significant premium brand; within a few months our UK case sales were running at close to 50,000 per annum and we were therefore close to Tanqueray and Beefeater and not far short of Bombay Sapphire. Only Gordon's maintained a huge lead, though we consoled ourselves that it was really a discount mass market brand and not a true premium brand like us.

When we bought Plymouth Gin from Allied Domecq in 1996, interest in gin was virtually non-existent. The drinks industry was having a love affair with vodka; gin was considered geriatric and boring. I like to think that we changed all that. Over the course of three short years Plymouth Gin became the fastest growing premium liquor brand in the UK market, and a renewed interest in cocktails and mixed drinks made gin an altogether more glamorous category. Almost overnight we started to receive solicitous attention from major drinks groups. One of the major Scotch whisky houses, for example, made a formal offer for our business; we were, tempted but thought we could do better.

IMPRESSING THE PILGRIM FATHERS

Charles and his small team had their work cut out servicing the UK market and maintaining the brand's momentum. However, we never doubted that our major opportunity lay in the US, a market that accounts for around half of the world's premium liquor sales. Initially we had thought that Plymouth Gin's success in the UK, the home of gin, would provide us with an invaluable endorsement to gain distribution in the US, but in this we were mistaken – the US market was a law unto itself.

From the outset, we had been anxious to form a relationship with one of the major US drinks importers or producers as we realised that even with the finest brand in the world, we would get nowhere in the US market without a strong distribution network. We made much of our UK successes in the US trade press and put out feelers to a number of potential US importers, but they were much less impressed with our brand than we thought they ought to be.

The only company who showed any interest at all was Seagram, as they did not have a strong premium gin brand in their portfolio. Their own domestically produced gin was, however, a huge seller. We knew them as rough and tough and difficult to do business with, but they were hugely powerful in the market. Clearly they were the distribution partners we really needed if we were to crack the US market. We met them in their swanky Manhattan offices a number of times to see whether we could do a deal for them to distribute Plymouth Gin in the US market but in spite of enthusiastic introductions from Seagram UK, an important subsidiary, whom we knew well, we made little progress.

They rather condescendingly told us that the UK market didn't really register on their radar screen, that US consumers didn't really care that the Pilgrim Fathers had lodged in our distillery prior to sailing for the New World in 1620, and that our new bottle and label design, though quite pretty, was insufficiently stylish for the more sophisticated American consumer. However, if we would like to give them our business for a knockdown price, they'd see what they could do with it, and they might even be prepared to allow us to keep a few percentage points for ourselves. They clearly saw themselves as kingmakers and didn't think they should help make the fortunes of a small group of foreign investors, that is, ourselves.

However, we did, meanwhile, make modest inroads into the US market, without their help, through a liquor distributor in Florida and also started initial sales in Canada, Australia, Japan, Scandinavia and elsewhere. We were nonetheless increasingly aware that, unless we could repeat our UK success in the US market, our progress would be limited. A new partner with real US clout was becoming a major priority. It was time either to sell out completely, probably at quite a low price, or form a long-term alliance with a serious player in the US drinks industry. A minor player just wouldn't do.

15

SWEDISH POLKA

*In which we did a deal with the Swedes that I thought would
solve our distribution problem and make us money in the
process, and a mad creation named Nigel got under my skin.*

One day I received a phone call from a director of N M Rothschild, the
London merchant bank. He explained that they had a client who might be
interested in buying Plymouth Gin – were we interested? I replied that we
may be but we would not entertain a silly, low price; nor were we interested
in selling out entirely as we would wish to retain some of the equity in order
to benefit from the huge future growth, which we knew could be ours. I also
said that we preferred to do a deal with another drinks company with strong
distribution muscle. We were not interested simply in a venture capital
arrangement; we wanted a partnership. Rothschild assured me that their
client was a wealthy company with powerful international drinks muscle.
Were we interested in meeting them? We most certainly were.

It transpired that the interested party was Vin & Sprit, a state-owned
Swedish drinks business, now part of Pernod Ricard, whose major asset was
Absolut Vodka, one of the world's greatest spirits brands. Charles and I met
two directors of V&S at Rothschild's offices in the City. We liked them at
once. They explained that V&S had received authority from the Swedish
government to raise money from the financial markets for acquisitions and
that they were determined to become a broadly based drinks business, a
Swedish rival to Diageo or Pernod Ricard.

At that time, in 1999, they were, in effect, a single brand company –
Absolut. They said they wished their first major acquisition to be another
white spirits brand, preferably a gin, and that they did not wish to get into
brown spirits for some time as such spirits – whisky, dark rum, cognac etc.
– generally needed ageing and the management of aged stocks of liquor was

not a skill which V&S possessed. They explained that they felt much more comfortable about making their first major acquisition in the gin sector as gin was a product which did not require ageing and which was a mixer drink, like vodka. With all such spirits, mixability, image and marketing were vitally important and this was what they knew. Were we interested in becoming part of V&S? They were clearly interested in us.

A FLYING PIG

But they had one other major benefit, which was particularly appealing and which had a delicious irony. Seagram, the US company, which had courted us but then proposed unacceptable terms, had the distribution rights to Absolut Vodka in the US and, it transpired, Absolut provided a huge proportion of Seagram's revenues and profits. V&S explained that if they acquired some or all of Plymouth Gin, they could deliver Seagram to us trussed and bound. If they instructed Seagram to handle Plymouth Gin in the US market, they would have no choice but to do so. In other words if we did a deal with V&S, we would not just gain a competent, wealthy, experienced partner, we would get serious US distribution immediately through Seagram, our US liquor distributor of choice.

We returned from our meeting at Rothchild's and conferred with the other shareholders. They were as excited as us. It was clear that price would not be a major issue and we all felt that we would enjoy working with the Swedes. But the icing on the cake was acquiring Seagram as our US distributors.

Richard Koch asked what price I thought we could get for the business and I suggested a figure which was over twenty times more than we had paid for it a few years earlier and two and a half times more than we had been offered some months earlier by the Scotch whisky business. He guffawed with laughter when I proposed my price and said he had just seen a pink pig flying past the office window.

I told him I was serious and that I really did think that Plymouth Gin was worth that sort of money to V&S. If they wished to get into the gin market, which they clearly did, we were the only serious brand around that they could plausibly buy. I had heard that V&S had been the underbidders in a recent auction of the Bombay gin brand, and were clearly disappointed at losing out to Bacardi. I said that they appeared deadly serious about buying our business and I believed they would pay top dollar. Not only that, they could justify paying top dollar because with Seagram handling the brand in the US, it could quickly become a million case brand and whether they paid us £5m or £50m, such sums would soon seem immaterial as the brand would quickly become immensely valuable. Charles concurred. It was agreed that Charles and I should enter into detailed negotiations with V&S.

A CONSENSUS

We met again with their directors at Rothschild's and told them our price. We also explained that we wished to sell only 50% of the business immediately and, in order to participate in the future growth of the business, wanted to sell the remaining 50% over the course of ten years at the rate of 10% every two years, with the value of each 10% tranche calculated mainly according to sales in the previous year. As we had rearranged the share ownership a couple of years earlier, so that Fred van Woerkom, Richard Koch, Charles and I were all equal 25% shareholders, this ten year buyout arrangement was a relatively straightforward arrangement for all parties.

The Swedes, we found, were careful and deliberate when making decisions. They were very like the Japanese: individuals do not make personal decisions, but convey proposals for consensus decision. V&S had a further complication in that, as a state company, they needed to get formal approval from state nominated directors on the supervisory board. Accordingly, it took several weeks from the time we put our proposal to when we finally heard from them. This was an anxious period for us. We had asked for a full price and for a buyout arrangement, which was a little unorthodox. Would the Swedes buy it? We had also insisted that we retain day-to-day management control of Plymouth Gin well into the earn-out period, arguing that unless we had responsibility for running the business, the earn-out arrangements would be meaningless. Would they accept these conditions?

I can remember taking a wonderful late autumn holiday that year in Tuscany. The weather was gorgeous and the countryside was at its best. I was reading a book sitting by the pool at a small hotel near Montepulciano when a long fax arrived for me. It was from V&S and my heart was in my mouth. But it was exactly what we wanted. The Swedes had accepted our price and all our conditions. It was simply now a case of drafting a detailed agreement.

This task fell mainly to Charles and it took several months. Every point was negotiated hard and then required ratification in Stockholm. But by early 2000 the deal was done and we were part of the V&S group. I remained chairman, Charles remained managing director, Richard and Fred remained non-executive directors and we acquired two new Swedish board colleagues, whom we took to immediately. We were raring to go and, in particular, couldn't wait to launch Plymouth Gin in the US market through Seagram. After all, that was the honeypot that could create huge extra value for all of us, including V&S.

A PROBLEM OF DISTRIBUTION

Unfortunately it was not to be. A few short weeks after our deal with V&S, we received a bomb shell – out of the blue, Seagram itself had been bought by a French company called Vivendi. It transpired that Vivendi was only interested in the company's media businesses and the Seagram drinks businesses were promptly put up for sale – the founders and major shareholders in Seagram, the Bronfman family, had diversified into various media businesses and these had become as important as the liquor businesses; it was the non-drinks media businesses that attracted Vivendi and led to Vivendi's takeover of Seagram and prompt disposal of their liquor interests.

So within just a few months of selling out to V&S, all our plans were scuppered and so too were V&S's distribution arrangements for Absolut in the US: it transpired that V&S had a clause in its distribution agreement such that in the event of a change of ownership of Seagram, they had the right to terminate the Absolut distribution contract. Once it became clear to V&S that Seagram was almost certainly going to be bought by a drinks business or businesses who already had their own premium vodka, V&S had no choice but to give notice of the termination of its distribution agreement with Seagram. Not only did Plymouth Gin not have any distribution arrangements in the US, nor did Absolut!

For much of 2000, the drinks industry was preoccupied with the auction of Seagram. Eventually, it was bought by a consortium comprising of Pernod Ricard of France and Diageo of the UK (the world's largest drinks company). Thereafter, all Seagram's brands were divided up between these two companies and Seagram itself ceased to exist.

V&S had been one of the bidders for parts of Seagram, but it never seemed to us that their bid was likely to succeed and it didn't. In due course, V&S formed a sales and marketing alliance in the US with Fortune Brands, owners of Jim Beam, and it also established its own import business in New York to handle the importation and brand management of V&S-owned brands, including Plymouth Gin. This new arrangement was announced in 2001 and was formally launched at a huge convention in Florida early in 2002. We had a foothold in the US market, but was it enough?

For most of the previous two years, we had been forced, frustratingly, to drag our heels. We could take no initiatives in the US or in most other major markets as the industry was in turmoil. In the UK home market our distributors, Seagram UK, were also being wound up and we thus faced huge uncertainty in every single market, as did our new partners and part owners, V&S. We had been full of expectations at the time of the V&S deal, but within a few weeks we were completely stymied.

All of us were immensely frustrated, but no one more so than Charles Rolls. He eventually sold all his remaining shares to V&S (Richard Koch did the same) and left the company. Suddenly the Swedes, who had by now acquired their first 10% tranche of shares, were 80% shareholders, and Fred and I found ourselves in a rather uncomfortable minority shareholder position.

We hired a new managing director, Nick Blacknell, formerly of Seagram UK, to replace Charles, and he did a good job for us, but Plymouth Gin was no longer a small, entrepreneurial business; it was part of an important state-owned liquor group. Nominally I remained chairman and Nick reported to me, but the real masters were now the Swedes and none of us could ignore this.

It was also becoming increasingly apparent that the Swedes wanted to run the Plymouth Gin business their own way and did not wish to follow the strategy which we had been following since 1996, and which I still fervently believed was the right one. In effect, they wanted to apply the 'Absolut approach' – modern, stylish packaging and lots of sophisticated advertising – rather than our approach whereby we focused on the product, the ingredients and the brand's heritage, mainly using the medium of PR.

BEING SEDUCED BY THE MAD MEN

We had never spent a penny on advertising and I had no wish to invest any of the company's funds in advertising until we absolutely had to. My view of advertising is that it is normally both expensive and wasteful and it is foolish to spend money on it if you can address your potential audiences in a cheaper and more effective way. In my view, the way for Plymouth Gin to reach its audiences continued to be through PR. Consumers believe favourable reviews by professional, well-informed journalists. They are generally much less convinced by advertising.

Not only that, in most sectors advertising budgets need to be huge if they are to create any impact at all. In the case of Plymouth Gin, a US advertising campaign focused on even a half dozen major US cities would cost many millions of dollars and even then would not be particularly powerful. I put this argument to V&S, saying that I might have been able to justify using advertising if I was selling professional aquarium thermometers, as, in order to reach my audience, I would probably need only to place a few full-page advertisements in the one magazine that all professional aquarium owners read. But whom do you advertise to in order to promote a gin brand? The brand owner needs to have an enormous budget and even then success is not assured. But V&S's faith in the power of advertising was unshakable.

It is true, however, that established and familiar brands often do not have the same ability to use PR as young, thrusting brands, as they are so familiar to consumers that their 'newsworthiness' is quite limited. But there is another more insidious factor that flatters the role of advertising. It is normally way easier for brand managers to spend their promotional budgets on advertising than on PR. If they follow the advertising route, they can have the fun of visiting the advertising agency in Covent Garden or Madison Avenue and being treated like young princes or princesses. They can be sure they will be dined in all the best restaurants. They might even have the excitement of attending photo shoots and meeting well known personalities. Advertising is an easy, glamorous, self-flattering way for companies to 'spend' their shareholders funds.

Spending even much smaller PR budgets is, by contrast, much harder work. The brand manager has to think up new stories, meet journalists, convince them there's a good angle, check press releases and generally graft. In the case of Plymouth Gin we used to organise dozens of trips to our distillery in Plymouth each year for journalists. On every occasion the journalist would be escorted, tastings would be arranged, the production process explained, and the history of the brand detailed. It was a gruelling process.

I was convinced – we all were – that Plymouth Gin needed to be built, in its early days, by a process of word-of-mouth recommendations, PR, tastings and contact with influential bartenders, not through advertising. This approach, however, was largely at odds with the brand building culture within V&S. Absolut vodka is essentially an 'image' brand and the image is communicated, in part, through the superb packaging but also through massive, attractive and expensive advertising. Indeed, advertising was so important a part of V&S's business model that they found it difficult to imagine how a brand could be built without it. We showed V&S what we had achieved in the UK and argued that this could be replicated elsewhere, but these arguments fell on deaf ears.

At our regular board meetings, this issue was debated repeatedly. The V&S directors did not understand why we would reject the large wads of advertising money they were prepared to hand out. I think they believed that we were somehow being small-minded in order to obtain maximum value for our remaining shares. They therefore came up with proposals whereby they would ring fence the advertising money such that advertising costs would not dilute the value of our equity.

In fact, this was not at all our concern. Rather, Fred and I felt that advertising would tend to alienate potential consumers who enjoyed the sense of having discovered this wonderful 'new' gin. Once the brand was advertised to all comers, it became less special. In addition, I disliked the idea of a large hole being blown in Plymouth Gin's balance sheet, even if there was no personal cost to us, and I hated, in principle, the huge waste that I knew advertising would entail and wanted no part of it. I felt that if V&S had money to throw away, I would sooner it went to Oxfam or Help the Aged.

HIS NAME WAS NIGEL, NIGEL BOND

Soon, however, matters were taken out of my hands. I heard through Nick Blacknell that our recently appointed New York importers, a fully owned subsidiary of V&S, had obtained a budget of several million dollars to advertise Plymouth Gin in certain US cities directly from Stockholm and had even appointed a huge US advertising agency to develop the campaign.

Even though I was chairman of Plymouth Gin, I had been told nothing of this. When I heard of it, I said I thought it was madness. The budget, though apparently huge and many times more than we had planned to spend on PR, was still, in my view, far too little to make any real impact in the chosen cities. I also believed that, in any case, the advertising agency in question was the wrong agency for a brand like Plymouth Gin, even had advertising been a sensible route to go. Their interest really lay in blockbuster brands spending hundreds of millions of dollars a year, not in a baby brand like Plymouth Gin. They were only 'handling' us in the hope that they would nab the Absolut account through a display of their advertising genius.

I spoke out strongly and, no doubt to appease me, I was asked to fly to New York a few weeks later to visit the advertising agency's Head Office to see their initial advertising proposals. I was assured these would be stunning, as the agency had developed an extremely exciting and novel concept. I would be massively impressed. All my former doubts and objections would be swept away.

We all gathered in a conference room in Manhattan and the advertising team presented their work. Their style was a mix of breathlessness and hucksterism. They said they had conducted focus groups among young drinkers (I didn't know these to be our primary audience!) and had come to the conclusion that Plymouth Gin needed a 'spokesman' and who better as a spokesman than a quintessential Englishman? They had, accordingly, developed a print campaign based around a fictional English brand ambassador. They also told us, with great excitement, that as we would find out a little later, they had even named this Englishman!

They then went on to show us press advertisements featuring an Englishman wearing a pinstripe suit and bowler hat, and carrying a briefcase and a rolled up umbrella. In each ad he was telling goggle-eyed American consumers about the wonders of Plymouth Gin. The Englishman was always shown with his back to the camera in order, they said, to preserve some mystery, but he always wore the same extraordinary outfit. He was, we were assured, a sort of James Bond figure, but he was not to be called James – that was too obvious – his name was Nigel, as Nigel was such a distinctive English name. They said they were quietly optimistic that Nigel would quickly become a cult figure in the US market.

When the presentation ended, all eyes turned to me. It was clear that my reservations had been widely broadcast. What did I think? Isn't this great advertising? Aren't we brilliant? Aren't you excited? Don't you think that the creation of Nigel is a stunning innovation?

I said that I thought it was one of the worst, silliest campaigns I had ever seen. I said it appeared to me that they had made no real effort to understand the brand, in spite of everyone having taken an expensive trip to London to meet British barmen and consumers and then down to Plymouth to visit the distillery. They had not seemed to learn anything about the 'texture' of the brand. I said that the campaign was absurd from beginning to end. I also asked them why they had chosen the name Nigel for the brand spokesman. Though Nigel Mansell had done something to rehabilitate this forename, I suspected that it was significantly less well chosen than they appeared to believe.

But when I voiced these objections I was rebuffed and told that if I didn't like the campaign then too bad – V&S's New York people had already approved the advertising and it was about to run!

There was, clearly, much glee at the prospect of my having to eat my words when the advertising turned out to be a resounding success. But, unfortunately, I was proved right. The advertising appeared, but made virtually no impact whatsoever. It failed miserably and only succeeded in wasting millions of dollars. Indeed, it was curtailed early.

It was almost a year before the inter-company charges came through from New York for this disastrous campaign. The costs were equivalent to about one year's turnover of the entire Plymouth Gin company and 40% of these costs comprised the fees, travel costs and other expenses of the advertising agency in coming up with the disastrous campaign.

Though at a personal level, the relationship which Fred and I had with the V&S team remained cordial; it was clear to both of us that there wasn't much of a role for two small shareholders like ourselves in a much larger business controlled by the Swedish state. V&S professed themselves to be anxious to use our skills and experience, but in practice they really wanted to run the business themselves and in their own way. They now 'owned the train set', not us, and wished to play with it.

Eventually, Fred and I proposed to V&S that they should buy us out completely and, in due course, this is what they did. We negotiated a fair price and it was probably a relief all round to clarify the ownership structure. For my part, it was a successful investment – in a few short years my return was well in excess of what I made during twenty years at Interbrand, and we were also well rewarded for the extra few years we remained as shareholders – but I could not help reflecting on what might have been.

In due course, V&S itself was put up for sale by the Swedish Government and was bought by France's Pernod Ricard. Interestingly, Pernod Ricard owned Beefeater so Beefeater and Plymouth were united once again. Pernod Ricard soon abandoned the swanky pack designs introduced by V&S and returned to the more traditional designs done by Interbrand designers. Overall, I had been able to put my branding theories into practice and my time at Plymouth Gin had proved to be great fun, as well as highly rewarding. But it was also somewhat frustrating.

But we were all fortunate to get out when we did. At the time we invested in Plymouth Gin, the gin sector was moribund. We were the only interesting game in town, though we had to work hard to get any spectators at all to watch our match. However, since 2000, perhaps 250 craft gin distilleries have opened their doors in the UK, US, Australia and other similar markets. Gin has now become the hottest spirit around. Consumer demand for premium and super premium gins has, as a result, grown quite markedly. But it is still quite small and very many brands are now competing for this limited market. Nowadays specialist gin bars (an utterly unknown concept only fifteen years ago) routinely stock 300 different types of gin. We did well to sell Plymouth Gin when we did.

Charles Rolls went on to help found Fever Tree, the enormously successful mixer drink brand, and Richard Koch has been one of the major early investors in Betfair, a huge internet betting business that has also enjoyed fantastic success. Fred van Woerkom and I, the two older guys who stayed involved with Plymouth Gin, have mainly gone on to enjoy our retirements, though we each remain involved in interesting businesses, both together and separately.

16

ST PETER'S BREWERY

*In which I use the proceeds of the Interbrand sale to become
a gentleman brewer in Suffolk, enter the world of mash tuns
and yeast recovery, and build a beer business from scratch
into an international, award-winning brand.*

The first thing I did when I received my payout from the sale of Interbrand was to build my own brewery and market my own beer. That brewery, called St Peter's Brewery, is, as far as I'm concerned at least, an unfinished story because I am still the owner and chairman, though any day some smart big-time brewer might press coin into my palm and add this brand to his portfolio. Meanwhile, it's my baby and it's fun. Let me tell you about it.

Most countries of the world have one (or more) internationally recognised brand of beer. Holland has Heineken, Germany has Becks (among many others), the US has Budweiser, Singapore has Tiger, New Zealand has Steinlager, Jamaica has Red Stripe and even the Bahamas has Kalik, a brand which I had a hand in creating.

A DETOUR TO THE BAHAMAS

My involvement in the Kalik project was in 1986. We had undertaken masses of work previously for Heineken, a company that was always fun and stimulating to work with. One day, I got a call from Thomas Haakkart, our main point of contact there (along with Mr Vellekoop); he asked me if I could go to the Bahamas for them for two weeks later that same month and, if so, I'd be briefed there. Not surprisingly, I discovered that I could.

It transpired that, at that time, all Bahamian beer was imported and Beck's was the preferred brand of the local beer drinkers. The Heineken brand came a good second. However, Commonwealth Breweries, the brewers of Heineken and a fully-owned subsidiary of the Dutch parent, had won the tender to construct a new brewery on the islands, thus providing local employment and reducing the country's import bill. In return, the Government would tax beer imports, so as to favour domestically produced brands. Heineken was, of course, happy with this proposal, but concerned that Bahamian beer drinkers might be upset if they were denied their favourite beer brand, Beck's, or if it rose steeply in price due to import tariffs. What did I think?

I studied their market research data and ran a few hastily organised focus groups, and quickly came to the view that they did indeed have an issue that needed to be addressed. My proposed solution: that we develop for them 'the beer of the Bahamas'. (There was no such brand at the time.) I assured them that this would fix the problem, as we could ensure that Bahamian Beck's drinkers transferred their affections to our new brand. They agreed with this strategy, but they wondered if I could develop such a brand for them in the remaining ten days of my visit! I was anxious about this too.

I ran more groups with consumers and quickly came to realise that there was no obvious, indigenous Bahamian 'culture' to which we could attach our new brand's imagery in order to give it local associations and affection and thus help it become the 'beer of the Bahamas'. Indeed most of the culture of the Bahamas was colonial in nature and not so very appealing to the average, male Bahamian beer drinker.

Eventually, a breakthrough! Junkanoo is the country's largest and most important cultural event and provides the Bahamas with a unique musical sound. There was, it was clear, only one area we could explore in order to develop our new brand, and that was Junkanoo. However, the name 'Junkanoo' was far too obvious to serve as a brand name for the new beer. I proposed, instead that we call the new brand Kalik, this being the sound of the cowbell, the unique instrument used during the festival.

Commonwealth Breweries, my client, was delighted and relieved. The kalik sound was utterly familiar to every Bahamian but had never been written as a word. Once it was turned into an 'echomimetic' name, it was recognised as strong and distinctive and unquestionably Bahamian. It was also available and 'registrable' worldwide as a trade mark. (The US market was of particular interest.) It was an utterly 'left field' solution, but was immediately accepted by management and, in the consumer groups we ran, by Bahamians themselves. Now Kalik is the unquestioned beer of the Bahamas. It is held in great affection and is also exported widely, particularly to the US.

This assignment gave me confidence – if I could help make Kalik a success, the future of St Peter's Brewery boded well too.

THE GREAT BRITISH BEER BRAND

Curiously, Britain doesn't have a strong international beer brand of its own, a British Kalik. Bass was one of the world's first power brands and may, just, still be the nation's leading international beer brand, but it would be lucky to appear in any list of the top hundred beer brands in the world. This is odd because Britain has one of the world's largest brewing industries, and the distinctive beers produced by British brewers and loved by British beer drinkers – bitters, pale ales, stouts, porters and so forth – are attracting increasing interest from beer drinkers around the world.

As I travelled around the world on Interbrand's business, I was constantly surprised at the lack of availability of British, and particularly English, beer brands. The diet of beer drinkers everywhere seemed to be lager, lager and yet more lager. Every product seemed to be just like all the others. In a blind tasting, I did not think that many consumers could readily distinguish Sapporo beer from Japan, from Brahma of Brazil or Moosehead of Canada; all that set these brands apart was their packaging and national brand imagery. I felt that beer drinkers everywhere would welcome full-tasting, differentiated, English-style ales. After all, if they were prepared to drink something as wacky as Guinness (Ireland's international beer brand) which they clearly were, why not English bitter?

THE QUIET BUSINESS OF BREWING

I had long thought about this as a business opportunity for myself, should I ever have the time and capital to pursue it. I liked the idea of making the transition from brand adviser to brand owner, and I was convinced that if I built an international brand of English beer, it should prove valuable. I also realised that, even though I could not afford to develop my own tyre or motorcar brand, had I been foolish enough to wish to do so, building a brewery and developing an international beer brand would, comparatively, take a relatively modest investment and one which I might be able to afford.

Finally, I believed that competitors in the British brewing industry would not go out of their way to throttle my new business at birth. It would be on such a small scale, it would hardly register with them and, in any case, none of them was really interested in international markets. Perhaps, I thought, I might be able to get on quietly with developing my brand and they might not notice my arrival until it was too late for them to do much about it except, perhaps, buy me out.

TRAVELLING BEER

But every time I thought about setting up a brewery, I was puzzled by one major issue: why was it that the British brewing industry hadn't gone international? I discovered that less than 2% of Britain's beer production was exported, and much of that at the time went to Calais to be taken straight back to Britain by booze cruisers. Holland, on the other hand, exported 70% of the beer it brewed. Why had British brewers turned their backs on export markets? Some of the answer lay in the nature of English beers. Cask ales do not travel well and have to be drunk within a few weeks of being brewed. But English beers can be kegged or bottled exactly like lagers, so this explanation could be only partial at best.

Eventually I came to the conclusion that the answer lay in the curious structure of the British brewing industry for much of the previous century. In most countries of the world brewers do not own pubs or bars. Indeed, in a number of countries, including the US, it is illegal for a brewer to do so. In Britain, on the other hand, brewers have traditionally owned huge pub estates. In the late 1980s, the majority of the 80,000 pubs in Britain were owned by the major brewers; Bass alone owned 8,000. The result was that the British brewing industry, unlike brewers in every other country, had never really adopted branding and a brand culture. The purpose of the Budweiser brand in the US is to persuade a drinker to go into a bar and ask for a 'Bud' rather than for a 'beer'. In Britain there was no point in a consumer going into a Whitbread pub to ask for a pint of Bass, as it simply would not be available. Therefore British brewers put their efforts into controlling their distribution via their pub estates rather than into building brands. But because they didn't have strong brands for their home market or real experience of branding, they didn't have the wherewithal to compete in international markets. Besides which, they were doing so well at home, why should they bother?

In the late 1980s the Government changed all this with the introduction of the Beer Orders, which drastically reduced the number of pubs any brewer could own. Companies like Courage, Whitbread and Bass were forced to sell off most or all of their pubs, and eventually almost all of these found their way into the hands of a small number of pub companies whose buying power squeezed the brewers unmercifully because they did not have strong brands with which to defend themselves. (No matter how much Tesco or Sainsbury might try, they still in the end have to stock Nescafé due to its astonishing brand strength, but no brewer had comparably strong brands to ward off the new pub companies.) Curiously, none of the British breweries turned to international markets to make up for the deterioration in home market conditions. Perhaps it was all too late.

FINDING ST PETER'S HALL

So this is where I found myself; having sold Interbrand in 1994, I decided to become a brewer of English beers and ales, and develop an international brand of English beer, the first of its kind. Indeed, I hoped to become 'the' international brand of English beer.

Though I viewed the new venture seriously and saw it as an opportunity to make a substantial capital gain at some point in the future, starting a brewery had other attractions for me. One of them was that I could set up my brewery in East Anglia, a part of the country that I knew and loved and where I wished to spend more time. It also gave me the opportunity to invest some of the proceeds from the sale of Interbrand in beautiful historic buildings and in good English antiques. Accordingly, I first bought a couple of historic pubs in North Suffolk and refurbished them with fine antiques bought at Christie's, Sotheby's and Bonham's auction houses.

All this time I was searching for a site for my new brewery. I knew that an industrial park would suit best, but I did not believe a brewery in such a location would fit the brand image I required – I wished to project my brewery as a craft brewery that brewed using traditional methods and the finest ingredients. Others could site their breweries next to sewage treatment works or oil refineries, but I wanted a rural location close to the fields where the barley was grown and with its own deep well for its brewing water.

Then one day I opened *Country Life* and saw an advertisement for a beautiful moated 13th century manor house near Bungay in Suffolk. I visited it the next day and thought it would suit my purposes ideally. It was in a remote, romantic location and had extensive farm buildings and a medieval thatched barn. I believed that the farm buildings would make an ideal home for my new craft brewery. The manor house itself dated partly from about 1280, but it had been extended in 1539 with earlier stonework and tracery windows taken from a nearby nunnery, after it had been dissolved by Cardinal Wolsey and Henry VIII. I put in an offer the following week and it was accepted within days. Within a few weeks I was the owner of St Peter's Hall.

Then, there was a period of frantic activity. I had already bought and was in the process of renovating the two ancient pubs, and I next acquired a fine country house hotel, all in North Suffolk. I also bought the lease on a historic pub in Clerkenwell, London, now the Jerusalem Tavern, and a favourite of all beer enthusiasts. Meanwhile I put out the word among the brewing fraternity for a head brewer – I also placed job advertisements in the brewing press. I received over eighty applications (almost one in ten of all the qualified brewers in Britain!), and found my man. In parallel, I recruited a managing director and, finally, I put in a planning application to turn the farm buildings at St Peter's Hall into a brewery.

I invested in pubs and a hotel, as well as in a brewery, because even though I disapproved of brewers owning their own pubs, I needed a few controlled outlets for my beer, as I felt it was important to have good 'shop windows' for my brand from the outset. I also needed to have some guaranteed production volume for the brewery until such time as the brand started to make progress in the home and export markets. In addition, I was convinced that pub freeholds were good value; if my brand needed further investment in the future, I could sell the pubs at, I hoped, a profit and reinvest the proceeds in brand development.

We brewed our first draft beer at St Peter's Hall in June 1996, about eighteen months after the decision to go into brewing and a little over a year after my purchase of St Peter's Hall. It was delicious. We now had a high-quality ale brewery, using water from our own deep borehole, and we were able to produce fine ales. But this was just the start.

ST PETER'S KEY AND THE RAVEN

While the brewery was being built, I had turned my attention to marketing and branding issues. The brand name proved a much simpler problem than I had feared. We searched the name 'St Peter's' in the UK trade marks register and in most important export markets and, miraculously, it was available everywhere. The company name therefore became St Peter's Brewery and the brand 'St Peter's'.

Our logo was developed in a similarly straightforward fashion. A couple of Interbrand's top graphic designers spent a day at the brewery and, while they were there, visited the local parish church. They noticed certain 18th century inscriptions had a ligature between the capital 'S' and the small 't' of 'St' in the name St Peter's. They therefore designed for us a logo that had a traditional typeface, along with the distinctive ligature. We also adopted a further graphic device incorporating a key and a raven; this was mainly for use on our bottle caps. We chose this bird because it was a symbol of the Vikings – the moat around St Peter's Hall had been built as a defence against the Vikings who raided the area frequently, prior to the Norman Conquest. The key is the key of St. Peter.

Another branding decision taken at this time was to have a single brand name – St Peter's – and to avoid the temptation to brand each style of beer separately. The reason for this was that we knew we had to brew a large number of sometimes somewhat unusual beers (for example, grapefruit beer, cinnamon and apple beer, honey porter etc.) as well as more conventional beers in order to get distribution, create consumer interest and win a few gold medals in beer festivals. If we gave a separate brand name to every variety of beer we brewed we would create a kind of 'brand soup'. We wanted to keep our branding simple and focused on one single brand name, 'St Peter's'. We therefore mainly used 'descriptors' for each of the different products.

But by brewing a number of different beers using unusual ingredients we were not at all breaking with tradition, as it was common practice up to the 19th century to add fruits and honey to beers to create special seasonal brews. Thus blackcurrant and gooseberry beers would be brewed when soft fruits were readily available, while at Christmas-time dried fruits, spices and orange peel would be added to create a special Christmas Ale. We were, therefore, in the mainstream of English brewing. It was the huge modern breweries with only one or two products that were out of step.

We now produce about eighteen different beers. Some are particularly popular in specific overseas markets (for example, Honey Porter in Finland and Gluten Free in the US), while others are used to provide market flexibility – if supermarket X doesn't want to compete on price with supermarket Y we can give each of them a similar but different product from our extensive range.

THROUGH A GLASS, DARKLY

A further major branding issue we encountered was that of our packaging. We knew we could never develop an international brand unless we produced bottled beers – cask ales do not travel well, and keg beer was not the image we wished to project. Besides, we might have been able to export draft beers to the US or Australia, but we'd never get the empties back. It was clear, therefore, that we had to go the bottled route; but what should our bottle look like?

The British glass industry offers, to small brewers like St Peter's, a range of entirely serviceable brown bottles, and these can be purchased relatively inexpensively. None of them, however, was, in my view, particularly attractive or distinctive. Moreover, I knew it would have been difficult to achieve real differentiation if we used the same bottles as everyone else in the craft brewing industry. Then, inspiration came.

During the course of a brainstorming session, my eye fell on an antique bottle that I had bought a few years earlier at the Olympia Antiques Fair in West London. This bottle was a late 18th century quart-sized bottle with a high shoulder and, most importantly, it was oval in cross-section, not round. Could we use this new shape for our new bottle? If we could, we would be able to market traditional English ales, brewed on an ancient site in a copy of an 18th century bottle. What brand heritage! What brand 'texture'!

This choice of bottle design has, in the event, proved to be both inspired and hugely problematic. Our oval bottle is attractive, distinctive and much loved by consumers. It is also absolutely unique, and we have been able to register it around the world as a trade mark. We believe that, over time, our bottle shape may well become as iconic as Coca-Cola's waisted bottle.

But it has also proved a major headache. In particular, running an oval bottle on a high-speed bottling line is by no means easy, and we have spent years learning how best to fill our bottles at high-speed. We also pay a premium for our bottles, as they have to be manufactured to more exacting standards than round bottles.

But our bottle has had one further, unexpected impact. My initial plan was to build a showcase brewery at St Peter's Hall and brew our low volume beers there. I planned, however, for our bottling to be done under contract elsewhere by third parties – we would not bottle ourselves. I also planned that, as volumes grew, some of our brewing would be contracted to third parties. We found, however, that relatively few British brewers have their own bottling lines (most focus on the production of cask ales), while those that do are none too keen on running an oval bottle on their lines, as the oval bottle requires special parts and much closer supervision. As a result, we have been forced to install our own automated high-speed bottling line at St Peter's Brewery, and have had to constantly expand production at this site. This has required frequent reinvestment and now our small showcase brewery is a relatively high volume brewery, something I hadn't planned for at the outset.

However, our bottle is, as I have said, much loved and performs flawlessly in the marketplace, as well as in our brewery and bottling hall. Recently, we have successfully introduced a round version of our original 18th century bottle and this is used for certain of our highest volume products.

A BEER FIT FOR A QUEEN

At the end of 1996 I showed our prototype oval bottle to the beer buyer at the huge Tesco supermarket chain, and he was very enthusiastic and supportive. He agreed to stock three of our beers nationally from early 1997, and for the next two years virtually our entire production went to Tesco. We had no spare capacity to develop export markets. Gradually, however, we have built up the brand's export presence and now around half of our beer production is exported to almost fifty different countries, but particularly to the US, Canada, Scandinavia, Russia and Mexico.

To my surprise, however, much of our attention has in the past been taken up with production issues and not with marketing issues. Can we speed up the bottling line? How quickly can we get new fermentation tanks installed and operational? How much water can we extract from our borehole? Marketing and branding issues have proved relatively more straightforward. I had thought that production would be straightforward, but I was wrong.

We have won scores of major awards for the quality and taste of our beers – we have a showcase full of them – along with Food and Drink Exporter of the Year award from Food from Britain and the Queen's Award for Export and now have devoted followers around the world, something which gives us all great satisfaction. It's a real thrill to receive messages from lovers of our beers in California, Manitoba, Oslo, St. Petersburg, Pisa or Tokyo.

St Peter's Brewery has therefore enjoyed unusual success and is well on its way to becoming a truly international brand of English beer. We export, proportionately, thirty or forty times more than the average British brewer and, arguably, are now the leading international brand of English beer, our key objective. It has not, however, all been plain sailing. It is twenty years since we brewed our first beer, so we have needed to take a long view. We have also sold our country pubs and our country house hotel and reinvested the proceeds in the brewery so as to further fund the business and provide us with an unequivocal branding focus. We have, however, kept one pub, the lovely Jerusalem Tavern near Smithfield in Central London.

A GENTLEMAN BREWER

St Peter's Brewery is a long way from Interbrand. Our head office and brewery is in a remote corner of Suffolk, not trendy Covent Garden, and, in almost every other way, the two businesses could not be more different. At St Peter's we have to watch costs carefully and every increase in turnover has demanded reinvestment. Our business conversations are about mash tuns, extraction rates, yeast recovery, health and safety, tachometer readings and bottling line speeds. Most of our staff have been with us for years and are drawn from the local farming community. A number of them have fathers or other close relatives working in the business. Recently we have set up a generous share option scheme and I hope that one day all our staff will receive a good windfall.

I believe that the time is approaching when we will receive an acceptable offer for the business (we have received dozen of unacceptable offers!), but the industry has changed hugely in twenty years. When I started St Peter's

Brewery, there was virtually no craft-brewing sector. We were pretty much on our own. Since then, the number of new, small breweries has exploded – we were one of only two or three in Suffolk in 1996, for example, but now there are well over thirty. Their combined volume is still quite modest, but they give the consumer massive choice. The same is true throughout the US and virtually every overseas market. Thousands of small craft breweries have opened up in the US, Canada and Australasia, most of them brewing English-style ales, not lagers. Portland in Oregon alone has now almost 200 small craft brewers we are told; twenty years ago it didn't have one.

The world's largest brewers, the natural purchasers of St Peter's Brewery (they have the distribution and financial muscle to turn St Peter's into a serious world brand – and there aren't many other small brands like ours around that could provide them with the necessary brand attributes), are still trying to come to terms, it would seem, with the huge changes taking place in world brewing. After all, there has probably been more change in the last twenty years than in the previous 200, and brewers have, consequently, never hitherto had to address change decisively. The innovative culture of the IT sector or of mobile telephony is utterly alien to brewers.

But this is changing; the large brewers seem at last to be coming to the view that they cannot any longer ignore major market developments, such as craft beer.

LOOKING BACK

As I shall explain, I got one important thing very right with St Peter's Brewery, but my handiwork was less confident in a second area. What I got right was the St Peter's brand and branding, but then it would have been disgraceful if I hadn't, would it not?

The main thing I got wrong with St Peter's Brewery was my mind-set. I didn't really see St Peter's Brewery as an altogether serious, profit-making business. I saw it as a hobby, a pastime to keep me involved during my retirement and which would provide me with an excuse to pursue various interests – vernacular architecture, antiques, branding, Suffolk, English ale and so forth. Sure, I wanted to make money – I certainly didn't want to lose any – but that was secondary. I was like a newly wealthy investor buying a vineyard in Tuscany because he liked Italy, the view, the food, and the wine, but who wasn't particularly interested in viticulture. Nor was I prepared to immerse myself entirely in the business. I allowed myself to stand on the outside, looking in.

Fortunately, I have realised this and taken the necessary decisive action. In particular, I now have found an outstanding new CEO, a much tougher task in rural Suffolk than I would have ever believed. Above all, I've learned that brewing is a very complex activity and needs the closest attention. To expect the brand, on its own, to lead to success was unrealistic. It does, however, help a lot. Now St Peter's Brewery is a great, but by no means huge business – we have a fabulous brand, a fine brewery, strong domestic sales – mainly through all the major UK supermarkets – and exceptional export sales. I have never been more confident of success than I am now. But it has not always been as straightforward as I had blithely expected. My confidence partly springs from a wonderful, unique alcohol-free beer, which we are planning to launch soon. Look out for it!

17

THE RUFFIANS

*In which I throw my hat into the ring of male grooming and
concule that our ambitions should start with a barber's shop.*

The third major branding business in which I have been directly involved
since Interbrand is Ruffians, a male grooming business.
Ruffians first saw the light of day in 2010-11. Andy Cannon, the son of fish-
farming friends from Oban in the West of Scotland, showed a strong interest
in brands and branding when we first met him in 2000. He was then in his
gap year between school and university. Later, having graduated, Andy took
a job in London working for a branded goods business and, in due course,
for an online retailer of branded fashion items. He visited us for dinner from
time to time, partly for a square meal, but also to discuss his latest brand
idea – he wanted to be a branding entrepreneur.

I found several of his ideas attractive, though each required significant
investment, and I doubted that he could raise sufficient funds to get any
of those ideas off the ground. Even if he did, I feared his stake in any such
business could be small. Finally, having discouraged Andy a number of
times, I put a counter-proposal to him.

This was to develop a strongly branded range of male grooming
products. I argued that this sector was growing fast and there seemed to
me to be opportunities in the middle to upper market sector. Moreover,
business success was likely, in my view, to be largely about branding.

Industry giants such as Unilever and L'Oreal seemed, I believed, to be
taking an 'eccentric' branding approach to male grooming products. Dove
for Men, for example, was being heavily promoted at major international
rugby matches, but Dove was, in my opinion, essentially a female brand.
Was Dove for Men credible to a male audience? Similarly L'Oreal's major
male grooming brand was L'Oreal Men Expert, another extension of a

women's brand into male territory, which I believed could be a stretch too far. These brands were 'quality mass market' brands, not upper middle or premium brands, but nevertheless they suggested, to me, that a bold new brand might be welcomed by the discerning male consumer.

I also suggested to Andy that the entry point to this market could be via a strongly branded barbering business. What better endorsement for a new male grooming brand than a barbering heritage? We could demonstrate clearly that we knew what we were talking about.

I put this suggestion to Andy and he said he would consider it. Meanwhile he married Cate and they set off on an extended honeymoon travelling around the Americas. I thought that would put an end to it, but I was wrong.

Some months later I received an email from Andy. He was approaching the end of his extended honeymoon and wished to talk further about the male grooming idea. Could we meet up in London on his return?

THE BRAND CONCEPT EMERGES

It transpired that Andy and his wife had given the proposal a great deal of thought. They had also sourced examples of interesting brands from a number of countries in South and Central America as well as from the US, many of which they had mailed for safe-keeping to Oban. He was keen to give the concept a go, but how?

MAKING IT WORK

We were all convinced that going down the barber's shop route was the best way to provide insights and credibility to our planned grooming products, but how might such a business get started? I had previously said to Andy that I was happy to help him set up a new business, but did not wish to become too involved – I was by then in my late sixties and felt my entrepreneurial days were over. He, however, had other ideas – and the more I thought about the business proposition, the more appealing it became. Accordingly, I agreed to help develop the new brand and the business plan, that is, to help him make the concept a reality. I also agreed to become non-executive chairman, to invest in the business myself and to try to find other investors. Andy, for his part, agreed to become CEO.

We worked together for months to develop a business plan, financial projections and the brand identity (name, logo, colour scheme; indeed, the entire get-up). We then formed the new company. The name we chose was 'Ruffians'. Next I spoke to two old friends about becoming investors too – Paul Stobart, formerly (of course) of Interbrand and Fred van Woerkom, one of the three investors in Plymouth Gin. Both said they were 'in'. We were now pretty much ready to go.

Andy had been born and brought up in Scotland and, though he knew London well, was not averse to spending a year or two in Edinburgh, a city he knew well but had never lived in. For my part, I was keen that we made any major early mistakes outside the glare of London, so was happy for us to trial our new barbering and product brand in Edinburgh, a small but sophisticated capital city, whose culture was similar to London's. The development of the business plan and brand identity, the forming of the company, the search for our first premises, the refurbishment of these and the job of developing a range of branded products and the packaging thereof took eight months overall, but by late 2012 we were ready to go – almost.

Our first major problem was that, only a week or so before the opening of our first store in Edinburgh, we did not have a single barber, not one. We had advertised, put posters in our windows, contacted headhunters and the job centres, and used word of mouth, all to no avail. A few possibilities had come forward, but no really strong candidates. It seemed that young, skilled, trendy barbers wanted only to work in the trendiest shops and we, an unknown quantity, were not yet trendy. However, Andy had had his hair cut in virtually every barbershop in Edinburgh (he couldn't grow it fast enough) and one barber, a young Australian, really impressed him. He had, however, told Andy he was not ready for a leap into the unknown. We held a board meeting in Edinburgh, just prior to our grand opening, and discussed our problem at length. What were we to do? We were desperate.

We decided our only option was to go back to our preferred candidate (for the third time, it transpired) and put it to him that he was foregoing the chance of a lifetime to join what was soon to become Britain's trendiest barbering and grooming business. Did he want to be 'the man who turned down the Beatles'? He relented and signed up. We opened with a single, full time barber, plus a couple of friends who generously helped us out for a few days.

ISSUES OF SCOPE AND RANGE

I have already mentioned, briefly, our plans for a branded product range and the development and protection of our new name, 'Ruffians'. In practice, these two programmes occupied a great deal of precious management time over the first year, as did the task of finding and opening our new barbershop. However, none of these matters could be put off until later and so had to receive proper attention from the outset.

Our initial range consisted of twelve branded products: shampoos, facial products, styling products and fragrances. Andy met with suppliers up and down the country. He also talked to packaging suppliers, both large and small. Eventually we settled on a medium volume, own-label supplier in Eastern England. We also settled on 'industry standard' packaging, as this was affordable and worked well on normal filling machines. We then finalised the pack designs and we were in business.

Four years and several production runs on, we are still happy with these products and with our packaging choices. All are excellent and several are outstanding. We also very much like our pack design, though, as we grow, we shall probably introduce physical packaging that is more particular to us.

Our trade mark programme was also prolonged and expensive. This was for one main reason: right from the outset we had planned to develop an international brand, not just a British brand. We wanted this brand to be able to embrace other up-scale products for men – clothing, fashion accessories, luggage and so forth – not just toiletries and fragrances and, of course, grooming services. Accordingly, we needed to find and protect a brand name that embraced a number of crowded trade mark classes and a lot of countries, including most of Europe, the US and Canada, the Far East and Australasia. We finally settled on the brand name 'Ruffians'. It had only a few relatively minor trade mark problems, all of which we were able to resolve, and, most importantly, it was strong, distinctive and appropriate. We were fortunate too in our choice of logo: a porcupine. (It was chosen by Cate.) It has proved to be internationally clear from the outset, and was also extremely distinctive. It has proved very appropriate – it is strong visually and the spines suggest a comb, essential in hairdressing and grooming. We filed our name and logo worldwide and, accordingly, have in place the key elements of an international brand.

PROGRESS

Within months our Edinburgh store was booming and good new barbers were approaching us every week, if not every day, to join our team. Our store design, pricing, range of services and products, store ambience, positioning and general store culture all proved to have great appeal, so much so that, in our first year, we won the 'Best Independent Newcomer' prize at the British Hairdressing Business Awards, the first time ever by a barber.

The next year, we opened in Covent Garden in Central London and here, too, we have enjoyed great success. About 70% of our business is now repeat, and we have received widespread acclaim in the media. Our Covent Garden store recently won 'Best New Salon' and 'Best Designed Salon' in the UK at the prestigious Creative Heads industry awards in a splendid ceremony at Tate Modern. We have since opened a second London store in Marylebone and are currently fitting out a third in trendy Spitalfields.

SO FAR SO GOOD

So our business is on the way, and Andy has proved to be a great CEO, but there is a long way yet to go. In the short term we plan to establish a chain of up to eight-ten barbers shops, all in Central London, and this plan is well on track. As we become better known to landlords, the task of finding new stores seems, fortunately, to be easing.

Already our attention is starting to focus on our branded products range, the main objective of our business. At present our range is only available through our own stores and via mail order. It is, however, proving very popular. It is, in our view, still too early for a national or international launch through upmarket retailers, but the time for doing so is approaching fast and we are now getting prepared. We are also launching branded clothing and accessories, following a successful trial, and are starting to appreciate the opportunities in these wider areas.

Of course, communicating with customers has been central to our success. PR has been the main way in which we have been able to reach out to consumers. Thus far the support and coverage we have received has been tremendous. All our PR efforts have come from within the company, not via external advisers. Fortunately, we have a key staff member who has proved to be exceptionally talented in this area.

FAMOUS LAST WORDS

Between us, the three investors have put almost £1 million into the business and Andy has invested a huge amount of time and effort. Will it pay off?

Of course, only time will tell. We have started well, but establishing a broadly based, premium, international male grooming brand is a highly ambitious project, much more ambitious than we had appreciated at the outset. We have laid good foundations, but there is a long way to go.

We have not trumpeted our ambitions for our brand, but nor have we concealed them. Recently, a regular at our Covent Garden shop said to Andy, "Come on. Tell me the truth. What's this all about? This isn't a regular barber's shop. What's the story?" Others too are taking notice and not just customers. A major world toiletries business held an international management conference recently at a luxury hotel outside London and one evening the delegates, fifty in all, turned up at our store in a luxury coach to have a look around. They later told us they were much impressed and that we formed a large part of their discussions the next day. We have also received approaches from Singapore, Japan, the US and Brazil, among others, for franchises or similar. We have politely rebuffed all such proposals, as we believe that we still have much to do before we embark on such arrangements. But we have made a great start and have been flattered, of course, by all the attention we have received.

18

MR KIPLING WOULDN'T LIKE THAT

In which I tell you the simple secret of brand building, both then and now.

Interbrand can, as I have asserted so many times already, claim to have 'invented' branding as a marketing and business discipline. Like any such invention, it was necessarily of its time. Had we expounded our views a decade earlier, we might well have been ignored, as the commercial world might not have been ready for it. As it was, our development of the concept of the brand, and of the discipline of branding, found a ready audience. And interest in branding seems to be at least as strong now as it was over twenty-five years ago. But much has changed.

Our view of a brand twenty-five years ago was quite prosaic and utilitarian. We viewed a brand as a business asset whose purpose was to enhance the earnings of the brand owner, make those earnings more reliable or both. We saw a brand as a product or service or business which had developed a personality that was appealing to consumers and caused them to value one particular product, service or business above others by forming a relationship between it and the consumer. We believed that brands were specific pieces of property that could be developed, nurtured, invested in, bought and sold, licensed or franchised to third parties and which needed to be properly protected in law. Branding was the entire process by which brands were managed, and we aimed for Interbrand, as the world's leading branding consultancy, to offer an exemplary service embracing all aspects of branding. Essentially we viewed brands as 'things' that had a persona and we observed that the best brand owners treated their brands in exactly this way. Their brands were not ephemeral, airy-fairy things. They were near tangible with their own strong, differentiated personalities and appeals.

MEETING MR KIPLING

I can remember an occasion when we were carrying out the valuation of Ranks Hovis McDougall's (RHM's) brands, the first such formal brand valuation ever. I was working on a portfolio of brands that included Mr Kipling, the famous British brand of cakes. In order to understand the brand better I asked the managing director of the RHM subsidiary that produced Mr Kipling products a series of questions about the brand. One area I probed was how easily the brand could be extended into new product areas, as this could have an impact on its strength and value. I asked him if the brand could be applied to a new hypothetical range of savoury products. "Good heavens, no," he said, "Mr Kipling wouldn't like that." Mr Kipling to him was a person. He had never existed and had never even been visualised, but to the brand guardian, Mr Kipling was a real personality who needed to be treated in a respectful and appropriate way. Mr Kipling was not a mere name.

Since the 1980s the concept of branding has been extended considerably. The first frontier after product brands was service brands. Then came business brands, then corporate brands and with these came the realisation that everyone in a corporation needs to live the brand. This led to the need for instruction, training and internal brand management and advocacy.

Soon marketing people were talking about branding cities, regions and even countries. Articles appeared in the marketing press on the branding of the Royal Family. David Beckham's advisers adopted branding techniques such that he now earns far more from the Beckham 'brand' than he ever did by playing football. (Andy Milligan has described this process in his entertaining book, *Brand It Like Beckham.)* Beckham's wife, Victoria, also understands the power of branding, stating during her early career as a Spice Girl that she wanted to be 'as famous as Persil...' As I know only too well, universities now also fret about their brand image. Indeed, every activity and enterprise seems to understand, however vaguely, that in order to succeed it needs to take care of its brand.

Interest in branding is not confined to a few affluent nations. Following the lead of companies in the EU, US and Canada, Japan and Australasia, branding has been adopted by Taiwan, China, India, Korea, the former Soviet Bloc countries, and emerging economies around the world. It is amusing to read indignant articles in Chinese business publications warning

Chinese businesses that they must protect their increasingly valuable brands to ensure that their owners' efforts and investment are not stolen by unscrupulous third parties in other countries. Not so long ago, on many street corners throughout China, counterfeit products were being openly sold that blatantly ripped off Western brand owners. The worm has turned, it would seem.

Many of these developments I welcome. Indeed, twenty-five years ago I was impatient for them to come to pass. But along with the development of branding has come a great deal of over-elaboration. Much of what is being offered by branding consultants today seems to be deliberately over-complicated. Every consultant wants his own matrix or proprietary methodology or analytical tool. Similarly, every business school throughout the world now seems to have a resident professor who has built his reputation on constructing an obscure branding hypothesis, which he has then branded as his own.

The purpose of consulting is to solve clients' problems. A good consultant makes the complicated simple, not the simple complicated, but this principle often seems to be ignored. Foolishly, clients quite often fall for it. Too many clients seem to think that if they don't understand a technique or presentation, it must be really good. So, beware the overcomplicated! If you don't understand what you are being sold it's probably the other side's fault, not yours.

BRAND MYSTICISM

A further trend, which I also dislike, is to view branding as a kind of religious or life-enhancing process. The argument goes that brands add to the texture of everyone's life. They permeate our souls in some way and thus have a mystical significance. Adherents of this belief go even further – the job of western civilisation is to bring brands to the benighted and unenlightened. By doing so, these wondrous creations of advanced western society will somehow release the shackles of poverty in the Third World and create a new Utopia. This mind-set sits comfortably with a belief in ley lines, pulsing energy sources from small pyramids, the healing power of copper bracelets and astrology. It is amazing to me that brands, things developed to benefit their owners, should have acquired such reverence.

In practice, branding's reach has expanded greatly over the last quarter century, but the fundamentals of brands and branding have not changed much at all; and a great deal of the increased sophistication of the brander's art is illusory. Marketing people are good at inventing flashy new words and phrases to describe the old and familiar. I would not wish to see the world of branding become as self-important as the world of advertising and would counsel everyone in the field to keep it simple. Just remember that a brand is a differentiated product or service or company with a distinct 'persona'. Treat it carefully and appropriately in order to reflect and enhance this differentiated persona.

19

MURPHY'S LAW OF HOW TO MAKE MONEY IN BUSINESS

In which I tell you the simple secret of making money, and it doesn't necessarily mean becoming an entrepreneur!

Creating and developing one's own business can be fantastic fun and, in a quite small proportion of cases, highly lucrative, but there are much easier ways of becoming wealthy than this. While it is true that some high-profile entrepreneurs, such as Bill Gates and Richard Branson, have made extraordinarily large fortunes, most entrepreneurial rewards are modest; indeed, very many entrepreneurs lose their shirts. If you are reasonably bright and emotionally balanced, and want to make money without sleepless nights or risking your home, I would recommend that you consider getting into the City, or joining a large corporation, becoming a civil servant or local government official, rather than adopting the life of the entrepreneur. These professions all offer good salaries, generous index-linked pensions, long holidays, plenty of sick days and relaxed codes of work – what sensible person would not head in their direction? But what would I do if I were starting over again?

THE CORPORATE TROUGH

Of course, the question is entirely hypothetical. The reason I started Interbrand was in order to escape the frustrations of the corporate world and the public sector, and I would probably feel these frustrations as strongly now as I did forty or fifty years ago. Another factor is that in the 1960s and 70s, the only route to serious wealth lay in starting one's own business. If you wished for security, a company car, a staff dining room, a reliable salary and a good pension, you would join a large company, but you would never accumulate a lot of capital. However, you would live comfortably and enjoy peace of mind.

Increasingly, however, 'organisation men' have arranged matters so that they enjoy all the comforts of corporate life and, at the same time, garner a fair chunk of the benefits enjoyed by successful entrepreneurs, without any of the risks. In the 1970s the chief executive of a medium-sized British company employing, say, 2,000 people might have a salary equal to ten or twelve times that of a secretary or a shop floor worker. Now that same chief executive probably expects a salary of one hundred times greater than that of lower paid workers. In addition he, or she, will expect stock options capable of generating millions of pounds of windfall gains. Men and women who choose to lead the corporate life take none of the risks of the entrepreneur, but often fully match the successful risk-taking entrepreneur in terms of the rewards they gain.

So my first advice to anyone wanting to become comfortably wealthy is to feed from the corporate trough or the public purse. It's a much safer way to go. Entrepreneurialism is high risk!

Not all corporate troughs are, of course, the same. The one most recommended in terms of financial rewards is probably financial services, but how does one get in to this sector? Well, first off, get as good an education as you can. Shortly after you're born you should prevail on your parents to put your name down for one of the best public schools so that you can join an elite club where members help each other out for the rest of their working lives.

Then follow it up by going to one of the better universities, preferably (in the case of the UK) Oxbridge. It doesn't really matter what you study, nor does it matter greatly what sort of degree you get; you can always explain away your honourable third in Icelandic studies by saying you were such a rounded person you decided to take full advantage of everything university life had to offer and didn't spend too much time on the academic stuff. People will think that you could have got a first if you had wanted to, but who wants to be a boring swot? You must next follow your glowing university success with an accountancy qualification from one of the big name accountancy practices. Such firms suck up thousands of bright, presentable young kids each year, but only have a relatively few vacancies for people in their thirties and forties. Most of their young recruits are, accordingly, birds of passage, but being able to say that you trained in accountancy with PriceWaterhouseCoopers or Deloitte's, even if you left as soon as you qualified, looks great on a CV and opens doors everywhere.

You might then consider investing in an MBA. This is not essential but can be the icing on the cake. But only go to one of the better business schools – London Business School, Manchester, Harvard, INSEAD or the like. Don't even consider Croydon or Bournemouth or South Shields, because even though they may be superb, they will look pretty second rate on your CV and might imply you're not a big league player.

You must be careful along the way to avoid tattoos, body piercings or a regional accent (apart from an east coast Scottish accent, which is reasonably acceptable) and, by the time you come to seek a serious job in the financial services sector, you should have invested, if you are male, in a good suit and, more importantly, an expensive pair of black leather lace-up shoes – no boots, thick rubber soles or 'Cornish pasty' shoes with Velcro fastenings. Never wear to the office any style of shoe that might be worn by a security guard or a copper on the beat, no matter how comfortable.

You should also use a good barber, avoid most styles of facial hair, cut your fingernails neatly, and ensure that your orthodontist provides you with a great smile. The rules for women are of course similar, but remember that female applicants are always slightly better placed than men at this stage of their careers, as interviewers are often male and many can't resist a pretty face, no matter how politically incorrect it may be to say so.

The purpose of these years of preparation is to land a lucrative job in financial services. To the cynical eye, many businesses in the financial services sector provide few benefits to society. After all, real wealth is created by manufacturers and farmers, not by those who manage pension funds, administer unit trusts, sell stocks and shares or play the money markets.

In practice, however, the rewards paid to those in financial services, and particularly those in the City of London, are out of all proportion to what can be made in true wealth creating sectors, making the rewards of headmasters and surgeons look paltry.

Of course, there are some very talented people in financial services, particularly in areas such as corporate finance, but most are no more or less talented than the rest of the population. They have simply fallen on their feet and found that part of the economy able and willing to pay hugely greater rewards than any other.

What is curious is that the rest of society goes along with it. Hard-headed businessmen do not seem to bat an eyelid when they pay a merchant bank its £50 million fee to help defeat a hostile takeover bid. Trustees of occupational pension funds do not seem to care that each of their pensioners averages a pension of only £5-6,000 a year, but the person managing the pension fund collects over £1,000,000 a year in salary and bonuses, even when the fund isn't doing too well.

So if you want to become very comfortably rich, my advice to you is to get into financial services, preferably in the City of London or in New York, Tokyo, Singapore, Dubai or some other such financial centre.

If, however, this does not appeal to you, you might consider joining the professions or a big business. Becoming a lawyer or professional accountant requires rather more intellectual horsepower than many other sectors and the workload can be punishing, but rewards at the top can be as stellar as in financial services.

However, an easier option for most of us is, as I have mentioned, to join a large corporation. If you get a job at a major business, and you have the right educational background, you are earmarked from the outset as someone destined for the top. You should quite quickly get into the big money and you can also start piling up the stock options. These can be particularly valuable.

In Britain, managers have talked for years about the fact that we operate in an international market place. Thus, they argue, British business needs to pay its executives the international market rate. Of course, the 'market rate' has been defined by managers at the American rate, which is the highest in the world, not the salary rates paid in Sweden or France or Japan, which are normally lower. Astonishingly, shareholders have fallen for this argument. Part of the reason lies in the fact that the voting power of shareholders now rests with pension funds and unit trusts rather than with individuals, and the managers of such funds, even though they are not the owners, are perfectly happy to see business executives receiving huge salaries, as it helps to justify the huge salaries which they themselves receive. Nonetheless, for a business executive from Barnsley or Surbiton to claim to be on a par with slick American executives from Silicon Valley or Manhattan and therefore deserving of similar rewards is somewhat far-fetched.

But because of the vigorous efforts of business executives in Britain over the last decades, the rewards of corporate life are now better than ever. They are also much more reliable than the rewards of the entrepreneur and pay much better benefits and pensions. So, if you have the stomach for it, consider the corporate life and forget about becoming an entrepreneur.

Of course, I failed to follow this advice in almost every respect. I was born and brought up in East London, not in an idyllic cathedral city in Southern England; I went to an appalling, brutal Jesuit grammar school in Tottenham, North London, not an ivy clad public school; and I studied at Manchester University and at an almost unknown post-graduate business school, Brunel, not at Cambridge or Harvard Business School. I also started my own business, as discussed earlier, rather than remaining in the soft world of big business. I have done reasonably well out of my choices, but do not own my own private jet. So what advice do I have for the would-be entrepreneur, that incorrigible individual who doesn't want to take the easy option and is determined to build a business for himself?

OPEN YOUR EYES

For a start, I think it is important that, in setting up your own business, you do it with your eyes open. I have known people who begin to take a close interest in classic car magazines and exclusive holidays just prior to starting up in business for themselves. They were clearly fixed on the huge rewards they think they will soon be making, whereas they should have been focused on the enormous problems that were bound to come their way.

Starting a business is extraordinarily difficult and highly risky. It is almost certain that you will need to hazard your home, as lenders may well not advance you a penny without collateral. And then, even if you do not actually go bust, which is always a strong possibility, you will almost certainly go so close to the wire, that for weeks you will not sleep properly and for the rest of your life you will remember those times with a sinking heart.

You will also be let down by people you know and trust. At times, you will have had to clean the offices and the lavatories yourself, as you won't be able to afford cleaners. You will travel in the cheapest possible way (there's no Business Class for budding entrepreneurs, only for the comfortable wage slaves), and you'll stay in the cheapest Travelodge or Formule 1. You will, even so, do well to survive the first few years, but, if you do, you will be lucky and will probably still make less money than if you had joined Unilever or Lancashire County Council.

Even once you become a seemingly successful entrepreneur, when times are tough the person who won't receive a salary is you, not the rest of your staff. But, in a very few quite exceptional cases, you could make a substantial fortune, though it's highly unlikely.

20

THE POWER OF MY BRANDS

In which I place my own three businesses under scrutiny –
how important is, and was, the actual or inherent power of
the brand to their success? What have I learned?

There is some element of 'the brand' in every business, though the importance and power of the brand varies hugely from one business to another. Thus for a City commodities trader the brand may rank pretty low down the list in terms of power and significance, while for Coca-Cola or Unilever their brands are, without question, their most valuable and powerful assets and the drivers of their success. Without their brands they would be undone.

This notion of the power of the brand is highly seductive to business people, and especially to branding consultants (like me), to designers, advertising agencies and their ilk. Indeed, increasingly consultants in the sector are propagating the view that brands are everything – get your brand right and all else will fall into place. You'll be successful, profitable, huge bonuses will come your way; you'll be on the pig's back until the end of time.

Seductive as this view may be, I've learned that it is not true. Even if you develop the most wonderful brand in the world, you may still suffer business failure. On its own, a brand can never guarantee business success; conversely, without a brand, business success may prove impossible. So, how important is, and was, the power of the brand to the success (or otherwise) of my three branded businesses?

PLYMOUTH GIN

When we acquired the brand from Allied Domecq we also acquired a distillery (on The Barbican in Plymouth), a head distiller (dedicated and competent), rudimentary business systems, a wonderful product, an existing get-up and packaging (though not so exciting) and a great heritage. There was however little distribution, no sales and little brand awareness. But the business and brand were not by any means 'naked'.

Accordingly, we did not need to set up a new business in a specialist sector from scratch. We could concentrate almost exclusively on 'core issues' – packaging, brand exposure, sales, distribution and so forth.

As a result, my perception of the importance of branding to this business may well be exaggerated. Yes, the liquid itself is of massive importance, as are production, distribution and so forth, but without a strong brand this business would have been dead in the water. The brand and its 'heritage' were accordingly, of critical importance but not of sole importance.

ST PETER'S BREWERY

I put a huge amount of effort into developing this brand and took a great deal of pleasure in the process. I put rather less effort into developing the company's business processes reasoning that beer had been brewed since the time of the Sumerians, so starting a brewery should be no big problem. Consequently, I left management disciplines and controls in large part to others.

As I have said, what was influential in my behaviour was that I approached the business with mixed motives. In no particular order, I wished to have the fun of developing a new brand, I wanted to provide employment in a remote corner of N.E. Suffolk where, at the time, unemployment was rife, I wanted to own and refurbish lovely old properties such as the brewery itself... and so on. And along the way I wanted, somehow, to establish a successful business and make money.

I therefore fell into the classic trap of the businessman who has made money in the manufacture of nuts and bolts or the design of cooling towers and then hazards it all, or much of it, by setting aside that which he had learned in his earlier successful career.

I knew in my heart I was tending to do this at times with St Peter's Brewery, but consoled myself with the (illusory) knowledge that a well-crafted brand would protect me. To a considerable extent it has, and now, fortunately, under new, skilled, well-informed and experienced management, the business is booming. But I have paid a price for my neglect.

I have learned the hard way that the brewing sector, especially in Britain, is much tougher and more complicated than most other branded product areas: there's the on-trade and the off-trade, tied estates, bottled beers, cask beers, keg beers, export, progressive beer duty, the supermarkets, the independents – the list is endless. And this is leaving aside health and safety, environmental issues, distribution, IT systems and other important matters. However, we are essentially a packaged beer brewery, mainly selling beer in bottles to supermarkets and export so have deliberately positioned ourselves at the 'brand intensive' end of the spectrum, even in an industry where branding normally plays only a bit part.

Most brewers do not have a brand with a fraction of the power of St Peter's and struggle mightily as a result. Indeed, many still think that advertising is the sole route to market success and are blind to the failure of such formerly massively advertised brands as Watneys Red Barrel, Trumans or Skol. Brands may not play the important role in the brewing sector which I had previously imagined, but without them you can be in deep trouble. The strength and appeal of the St Peter's brand and the powerful bond it has with consumers has allowed the company to thrive even in relatively tough trading conditions. Indeed, I know that St Peter's is one of the strongest brands there is in brewing, and we shall increasingly benefit from its power.

RUFFIANS

Well, time will tell, the jury's out, I'm holding my breath, it's in the hands of the gods – what can I say? I'm confident of the success of this new brand but we must wait and see. I'm sure we've done a fabulous job of brand development, that we have a skilled and dedicated CEO and Board, a good business idea and a dedicated, hard-working and talented team, but predictions as to future success can be dangerous.

Clearly, however, brand strength is absolutely critical to business success even though other factors will also play a powerful role, particularly our decision to launch our new male grooming brand via the barbershop route.

We all believe, therefore, that the approach we have taken to building the Ruffians brand will pay off handsomely, and that, in future years, Ruffians will become a major international brand of male grooming products with deep roots in fine barbering. It's a bold way to go, but I, and all the others behind the brand, have faith in what we are doing.

VARIATIONS

So the role and power of the brand differ in each of the branded businesses in which I have been involved. But brand power is of key importance in each instance.

FIFTEEN SIMPLE RULES FOR BUSINESS SUCCESS

If this hasn't put you off, how do you go about becoming a successful entrepreneur, whether a branding entrepreneur or any other type? Here are my fifteen rules, not all of which I've slavishly followed; though when I haven't, I've normally lived to regret it.

1. First, you need passion. You want to work for yourself and to control your own destiny. If you don't have this, you should opt for the corporate life.
2. Next, you have to find an entrepreneurial or branding niche for yourself; in other words, you have to come up with 'the idea'. There's no point in starting a business exactly like others out there in the market place already. So give customers a reason to choose you or your brand rather than your competitors. In other words, be different. This differentiation can lie in a small detail of the service or product you provide – printing your business newspaper on pink rather than white paper might provide sufficient differentiation – but it must be noticeable to consumers, sustainable and appealing.
3. Your idea or brand should, if possible, be legally protectable. Once you have created a success, others are sure to try to copy you and the most likely way will be by offering virtually the same product or service but at a lower price. So, protect your idea in some way. This can take the form of trade marks, patents, copyrights, exclusive know-how, proprietary formulae, strong visual branding, unique distribution arrangements, well-located premises – the list is endless, but do something, and try to make sure it's effective.

4. Be truly innovative. Many of the products and services we accept today as being the norm were considered quite wacky when they first appeared. Nobody believed such an idea could fly. A service naming new products is one example; others are health clubs and high street coffee bars. Remember that British consumers thirty years ago scoffed at the idea of buying bottled water when they could get all the water they needed from the tap for nothing. So don't dismiss out-of-hand setting up a business offering an innovative and superior window cleaning service or a peach-flavoured sake drink. Just because such things are not on the market at present doesn't mean they can't be a success in the future.

5. If you are successful, consider how your business might be scaled up. If your wonderful new window cleaning service does well, how do you turn it into a regional, national or international business? After all, you probably don't want to clean windows all your life. You might, therefore, consider franchising your concept or opening branches elsewhere. You will need to have at least a vague notion at the outset as to where you're going and ensure that the basics of a franchisable or expandable business are put in place, right from the beginning. Often this comes down, as ever, to protectable elements in your business concept, which you can exploit more widely should you so wish.

6. Choose a concept that doesn't ruin your life. If you wish to set up a business providing services for weddings, accept that you'll never have a free weekend again.

7. Select a business with healthy margins. Running a business on thin margins is difficult and stressful, and you will always tread a fine line between survival and disaster.

8. Another pitfall to avoid (I have often failed to do so) is that of giving away too much of the equity at the outset. I have found that men, in particular, find the notion of setting up entirely on their own quite difficult and lonely. They enjoy the companionship of working with others and more often than not envisage some sort of shared co-operative activity, even when it is clear that only one person will be driving the show – you. Don't give it all away before you start. You can, if necessary, be generous later.

9. Be prepared to live your new business night and day. Businesses are not like bedding plants. You don't stick 'em in and come back three months

later to find out whether Mother Nature has done her stuff. You must be involved in every single detail. You can't afford to say, 'I'm not a numbers person', or 'I don't understand the production side'. You have to become intimately involved in every single aspect of the business.

10. Set high standards from the outset in every aspect of the new business and refuse to compromise on them, whatever the pressures to do so.

11. Be assertive. The chap in the corner who is always huddled over his computer screen may well be working, but he could equally be sending e-mails to his girlfriend, buying music online, or even looking at pornography. He may appear to be working hard but if he isn't, it's your time and money that he's wasting and your business that he's damaging. You should not, therefore, feel bad about walking around his desk and looking over his shoulder at what's on the screen. If he turns it off a microsecond before you get there, it's probably not because he's shy, but because he's guilty. You are paying his salary, you should remember. What's happening is in your time, so be assertive. Nor should you hesitate to check expense claims from directors and other staff members, otherwise you will almost certainly be ripped off – and often by the most unexpected people.

12. Never, ever allow anyone to have a company credit card as these are always abused. Indeed, I think they are evil. The charges on such cards come directly to the company, thus avoiding the normal screening process, and the resulting lack of accountability always leads to abuse, often significant abuse. This is not just confined to those in the private sector. I have known a university vice-chancellor who misused his corporate credit card on a grand scale. Once spent, it can be very, very difficult to re-coup the sums that have been misappropriated. So if you are ever pressured to agree to a corporate credit card, refuse. Perhaps you could offer a 'float' instead? And never have such a card yourself. Also, forbid your staff to fly Business Class at your expense, or stay in luxury hotels. They'll think up every reason under the sun why they should (e.g. 'It'll look bad to XYZ if I don't', 'I need to get to the meeting in the best possible shape', etc.) but if they don't travel this way at their own expense (they won't, you can be sure), they should not do so at yours.

13. The best businesses are always the simplest. Avoid over-complicated systems and over-elaborated ideas. If you can't explain to the uninitiated

what you do or plan to do in less than two minutes, there's probably something wrong. Far too many people think their business concept is 'smart' if their business plan is full of complication and buzzwords. In fact the reverse is true.

14. The intensity of your own business is something that you should be prepared for. If your new business is to be successful, it will engage you at every level. You must be passionate about the product or service you are offering. But it goes beyond this. Your new business will bring you more fun and more excitement, but also more lows and disappointments, than any other activity. In particular, you must be prepared for the fact that people in whom you place immense trust and whom, you are quite certain, you have treated with great generosity, will let you down. You may find that someone has been fiddling his expenses or receiving kickbacks from suppliers or plotting to set up in competition, and if this happens, the feeling of let down and hurt is intense. Be prepared for this. And be prepared to be on call seven days a week – a civil servant may enjoy a 35-hour week, but you won't.

15. Finally, if you are successful, most people will play down your achievements. 'He – or she – was lucky'. 'It's a matter of being in the right place at the right time'. Nobody except you will really know the risks and efforts involved in creating a successful business. It may look so easy to anyone who has not been through it. But it isn't.

OUR CHANGING TIMES

In my experience, entrepreneurialism has always been applauded in the US, but less so in Britain. In the mid 1970s, when I founded my business, I quickly realised that to tell anyone at a dinner party that I was starting a business was usually a major faux pas. They would quickly change the subject or break off to talk to the diner on their other side. Working in business at all was considered by many to be pretty grubby (even though the fortunes of many of our 'betters' were in fact derived from the slave trade or from sending miners down criminally dangerous pits for very low wages). Being an entrepreneur was especially grubby. It was much the same as being a street trader or a bookies runner.

Fortunately, entrepreneurs have come up in society over the last thirty years, and now business schools teach entrepreneurship, politicians applaud SMEs (small and medium sized enterprises) and local authorities build starter units for small businesses on new business parks. Indeed, there is recognition that new businesses are the life-blood of our economy and of our entire society. So things are heading in the right direction for us entrepreneurs. But there's still a way to go.

Finally, virtually every business is, or contains, a brand. Some contain many brands – and such brands are hugely valuable assets. You must be sure to nurture your brand or brands. You must take great care in their creation, development and protection. You must not allow your staff to 'play' with them, as they would love to do, and nor should you allow third parties unauthorised access to them. Neglect your brand or brands at your peril.